Creative Demons
And How to Slay Them

Creative Demons

And How to Slay Them

Richard Holman

ILLUSTRATED BY AL MURPHY

For Loop, Blue & Beau

First published in the United Kingdom in 2022
by Thames & Hudson Ltd, 181A High Holborn,
London WC1V 7QX

First published in the United States of America
in 2022 by Thames & Hudson Inc., 500 Fifth Avenue,
New York, New York 10110

Creative Demons and How to Slay Them
© 2022 Thames & Hudson Ltd, London

Text © 2022 Richard Holman
Illustrations © 2022 Al Murphy

Designed by Fraser Muggeridge studio

British Library Cataloguing-in-Publication Data
A catalogue record for this book is available from
the British Library

Library of Congress Control Number 2021943302

ISBN 978-0-500-02460-7

Printed and bound in Latvia by Livonia Print

MIX
Paper from
responsible sources
FSC
www.fsc.org   FSC® C002795

Contents

From the point

who creates,

is a

a *leap*

of view of one

everything

gamble,

into the

unknown.

Yayoi Kusama

Introduction

Take a room full of 5-year-olds, give them some pens and paper, then ask them to draw whatever they like. Pretty soon you'll have a pile of gloriously original artwork. Some of the drawings will resemble physical objects. Others will be completely abstract. A few will just be colourful scribbles. But all the kids will have created something.

Now take the same kids ten years later. Same room, same pens and paper, and the same task. The results will be very different. The 15-year-olds will be way more hesitant. They'll probably ask you to give them some kind of steer. They'll look around awkwardly to see what everyone else is doing. If you're lucky, a couple of them will set about the task with gusto. More likely, they will tell you they can't even begin because they can't draw.

What happened?

Where did all that carefree creativity go?

It's a truth often remarked upon that creativity isn't learned, it's unlearned. The older we become, the more we question our ability; the more we cast an envious gaze over the work of others and think, 'I could never do that'; the more fearful we are of making mistakes, of being seen to look a fool. And so, slowly, over time, each of us develops our own pernicious cadre of creative demons.

It is your creative demons who slyly suggest that when it comes to writing the first chapter of your novel, tomorrow is going to be a better day to begin than today. It is your creative demons who tug at your hand, creating that irresistible force that stops you making a mark on the blank canvas before you. And the little voice that whispers in your ear in the dead of night that you're a talentless pretender with no conceivable hope of making anything of any worth? That's a creative demon.

Here are three things you need to know about these bothersome beasties who would seek to frustrate your creative impulses at every turn.

The first is that no artist, writer, musician, performer, thinker or maker is without them, no matter how talented, successful or acclaimed they may be. As you'll discover in these pages, some of the greatest names in human endeavour have had to fight long, hard, treacherous battles against their own creative demons: Leonardo da Vinci, J.K. Rowling, Dr Seuss, Brian Eno, Herbie Hancock and Marina Abramović – all have been afflicted, yet all have overcome.

The second is that the longer you leave your demons unchecked, the more they will thrive and the bigger they will become. Fail to confront them and they may completely overwhelm your creative impulses. Self-doubt, indecision and fearfulness will paralyse you, and that triumphant, life-affirming feeling of stepping back from the lyrics you've just written, the pot you've just thrown or the image you've just drawn and thinking, 'I made that!' will never be yours.

Finally, the third thing you must know is this: no matter how hairy, grotesque, bloody-minded or downright noisy your own personal creative demons are, they can be vanquished. Sometimes, as we'll see, they can even be put to good use.

The world needs your creativity now more than ever. We need original thinking and innovation to help us solve the problems that we human beings and all the other species on our planet face. We need books, plays, movies, music, theatre and art to unite us and help us make sense of what it means to be alive today. And each of us needs to be able to indulge in losing ourselves, for just a little while at least, in the comfort of bringing something into being that didn't previously exist.

So come with me on this quest to hunt down the most devilish of all the demons, one by one. Give me your time and I'll show you how, with cunning, conviction and a little bit of help from some of our greatest creative minds, you can overcome your own mind-forged monsters and start making.

Chapter 1

The Demon of Procrastination

Faire

se

*Just shut up and do it

et
*taire**

Gustave Flaubert

I have a confession to make: I've been putting off writing this chapter for a long time. Putting off a chapter about procrastination... I guess you could call it method writing.

Even now, as each word reluctantly appears on my screen, I notice how dusty the corner of my desk is. The Demon of Procrastination purrs in my ear, 'Hey you, maybe this whole writing thing would work out better with a clean desk? And those pencils look a bit blunt too. Why not get them nice and sharp and crack on tomorrow? Oh, and when was the last time you checked Instagram?'

It's easy to think of the Demon of Procrastination as a rather innocuous creature. All he's asking you to do is delay putting pen to paper or brush to canvas until tomorrow. He's not saying never, is he? But how many poems, plays, paintings, even entire artistic careers, have been lost to his beguiling ways? The seconds become minutes, the minutes become hours, and – before you know it – the hours have become years.

The Demon of Procrastination draws his maleficent power from the dark pool of your personal and private fears.

There is the fear, shared by anyone who ever tried to create anything exceptional, that you're just not up to the task in hand. The feeling that you're an impostor, a pretender, a deeply deluded soul who will be unveiled the moment you attempt to transform your dream of being a writer or painter or performer into a reality.

There's the fear about the work you hope to produce. What if it's no good? What if it's worse than no good and makes you look ridiculous for imagining you had any creative talent in the first place?

Then there's the fear that the journey itself, from writing the first line to placing a full stop on the final scene, will be too arduous. You look around you at the creative works you admire – the novels, the plays, the movies, with all their exquisite detail and intricate refinement – and think it's going to be too damn hard.

So you put the whole thing off until tomorrow.

And the dream remains a dream.

To defeat the Demon of Procrastination, we must confront the fears on which he feeds, one by one. So what of the first, the fear that you're nothing more than a pretender?

Well, you may find it reassuring to know you are not alone. To delve into the biographies of any of our most esteemed creators is to discover that almost all of them have, at different points in their lives, been on intimate terms with self-doubt. If you are an artist, you are someone who is particularly attuned to what it means to be human. And one of the truths of what it means to be human is that somewhere along the way, on our journey through life, we're bound to lose faith in ourselves.

One of the masterpieces of 20th-century fiction is *The Grapes of Wrath* by John Steinbeck, first published in 1939. It's a tale of loss, heartbreak and endurance set against the backdrop of the Great Depression in America. The novel won the Pulitzer Prize and was instrumental in its author being awarded the Nobel Prize for literature. It has become a classic. Yet, as he was writing it, Steinbeck confessed his doubts privately in his journal: 'I'm not a writer. I've been fooling myself and other people. I wish I were... no one else knows my lack of ability the way I do.' This was not a temporary lapse of confidence. Almost every hard-won page of his magnum opus was a soul-sapping struggle against the feeling of his own inadequacy.

Few would question the accomplishment of the painting on the vault of the Sistine Chapel in Rome, perhaps one of the greatest artistic achievements of all time. But its creator Michelangelo did. Midway through, the artist wrote a poem to his friend Giovanni da Pistoia describing his struggle: 'My painting is dead... I am not in the right place. I am not a painter.'

There are really only two kinds of successful creators – those who admit to insecurity and those who deny it – but everyone experiences it. It's a prerequisite of being good. To be free of self-doubt is to lack the critical acuity you'll need when it comes to evaluating and refining your work. The trick is to avoid letting your insecurity stop you from producing the work in the first place.

Remember that no matter how ill at ease you may feel with your own flaws and limitations, you are in a very privileged position. No other writer or artist sees the world as you do, because no other writer or artist is you. As Dr Seuss once sagely wrote, 'Today you are you! That is truer than true! There is no one alive who is youer than you!'

You're only a pretender for as long as you're pretending to work. Pick up your brush and paint, and you become an artist. Pick up your pen and write, and you become a writer. And don't let anyone tell you otherwise.

What of the second of our fears, that it's fruitless to attempt to outwit the Demon of Procrastination because, even if we do produce any work, it's bound to be a disappointment?

When a creative idea is just an idea, it's untainted by the prosaic demands of execution. It's soaring, beautiful, perfect. Naturally, you're afraid that if you try to bring that idea into being, you'll be faced with all kinds of practical challenges that must inevitably diminish it.

And you're absolutely right.

There's no way to sugar-coat this particular pill.

Your first draft or first sketch will, probably, suck. Maybe it will feel derivative, too close in style to the work of your heroes. Perhaps it will seem clumsy and blunt, with an apparently unbreachable distance between the insight that inspired you and the insipid rendering now before you. Almost certainly it could be simpler.

But at least you have something. Something to work with. Some lines, some words, a series of notes that had never been put together before you put them together today. Of course, if you compare this first draft to the classics in your genre, it will come up pitifully short. But remember: those masterpieces you're judging your own imperfect efforts against may well have begun life in an equally meagre state. Their creators have crafted, refined, tweaked and redrafted them, and you will be able to do the same to your own work too, once it exists as an object in its own right.

If you set out with the intention of creating a masterpiece, you may as well hang a welcome banner over your door inviting the Demon of Procrastination to come on in. The empty vanity of making work purely for acclaim or approval is unlikely ever to carry you beyond that first hurdle of discovering your own failings as an artist.

Yet if you accept that you're going to begin by making something that's not great, that may even be pretty terrible, then it will be a whole lot easier to get started.

I used to work as a creative director in the world of design and advertising. On those occasions when my team and I needed to come up with a good idea quickly, when the clock was ticking loudly in the corner, I'd ask them for the worst possible idea they could think of in response to the brief. The mood would switch immediately. With the quality-control filter switched off, ideas would flow. We'd relax, laugh, have fun. And pretty soon we'd stumble, almost by accident, into a really fruitful concept. If you want to begin, set the bar low.

What of the third fear to fuel the Demon of Procrastination, the expectation that the creative journey will be too overwhelming?

Well, you know that old expression of not being able to see the wood for the trees? When it comes to getting started on a creative project, it's okay not to be able to see the wood. In fact, it's better not to think about the wood at all. It's too big, too dark, too unknowable. Instead, pick a single tree. Get close to the tree, examine it, explore it and start there.

The only way Steinbeck got through the pain of producing *The Grapes of Wrath* was to set himself the task of writing it line by line, page by page, day by day. To consider the whole was too daunting. He showed up at his desk and got a few words down daily, whether he felt they were any good or not.

There's a great line by the American novelist E.L. Doctorow about the process of writing being 'like driving a car at night. You never see further than your headlights but you can make the whole trip that way.' Don't worry if you're unsure of your destination – when it comes to the creative process, this can be an advantage. As the artist Bridget Riley observed, 'People feel that it is very important for artists to have an aim. Actually, what is vital is to have a beginning. You find your aim in the process of working. You discover it.'

As an artist or writer, the responsibility for building momentum in your work lies with you. You'll probably feel an inertia born of fear, doubt, laziness, whatever – this you have to overcome. Initiating the process is often the part that requires the most effort, like spinning a large wheel. But once you've generated some momentum, you may find that the work itself carries you somewhere you could never have expected, perhaps somewhere even better than you imagined.

If you're really lucky, there may come a time when your characters write themselves, when the melody flows through your fingers without you knowing where it's coming from, or the painting appears on the canvas in front of you, almost as if you're not there. When this happens, it's a kind of creative nirvana. The world falls away and you're lost for a moment in something bigger than yourself. As a creator, this feeling is as good as it gets (and it's one we'll return to in later chapters); it will more than make up for those countless hours of bruising self-doubt. But give in to the Demon of Procrastination, allow it to feed on your fears, and this rare and glorious ecstasy will never be yours.

So what's it going to be?

Are you going to continue to let this particular demon squat on your shoulder, whispering his hollow distractions in your ear?

Or is now the time to knock him off and take the first step on your creative journey by simply putting one foot, or one word, or one brushstroke, in front of the other?

Chapter 2

The Demon of the Blank Page

If I knew
where the
good *songs*
came from,

I'd go there
more
often.

Leonard Cohen

To be an artist is to confront some of life's most fundamental questions...

Who am I?

Why are we here?

And where the hell did all my good ideas go?

The Demon of the Blank Page is a capricious creature who strikes mercilessly, with no regard for the dedication, ambition or past achievements of his victims. Where you will encounter him you cannot predict, but if you choose to engage in a creative pursuit, sooner or later your paths must cross.

When Dylan Thomas was at the height of his fame, in the late 1940s and early 1950s, packing out theatres and concert halls across the USA and enjoying the kind of international success that few other poets have ever known, he became paralysed creatively, writing just six poems in six years. As I write, my son is downstairs reading *To Kill a Mockingbird* by Harper Lee, a Pulitzer-winning novel enjoyed by tens, maybe hundreds of millions of readers since its publication in 1960. Yet Harper Lee was able to publish only one other novel in her long lifetime, and that was said to have already been drafted before her masterpiece. In a letter to his brother Theo, during a particularly barren patch, Van Gogh wrote, 'You don't know how paralysing it is, that stare from a blank canvas that says to the painter you can't do anything. The canvas has an idiotic stare, and mesmerizes some painters so they turn into idiots themselves.'

And if you're wondering whether a lack of inspiration can strike musicians, take a look at the list of the longest gaps between albums on Wikipedia. The lesser-known Sonics top the charts with a gap of forty-eight years but not far behind are Chuck Berry, The Stooges and the Pixies, all of whom kept their fans waiting for over twenty years between releases.

The Demon of the Blank Page has driven some of our most famous creators to the edge of despair – and in some cases, beyond. No one is immune to his influence. The troublesome truth about this demon is that the more you battle with him, the more desperate you become; and the more desperate you become, the harder it is to have a good idea.

If we're to prevent this mercurial miscreant from blocking our path and derailing our creativity, we must first address a daunting question: where *do* good ideas come from?

To find the answer we'll need to take a trip inside your brain.

We used to understand the brain in terms of its two hemispheres. The left hemisphere was thought of as the serious, grown-up part of the brain – the home of critical, rational thinking as well as language. The right hemisphere was the hippie next door: abstract, artistic, intuitive – all mandalas and patchouli oil.

Thanks to countless hours of hard work by neuroscientists and the development of techniques to record brain activity with intimidatingly long names like functional magnetic resonance imaging (fMRI) and high-density electroencephalography (EEG), we now know that the truth is a little more complex. The estimated 86 billion neurons in your brain network together, often across hemispheres, in a myriad of different ways depending on what you're doing.

A much better way to think about, erm, the way we think is to recognize that there are two principal modes of thought: the analytical and the spontaneous.

Analytical thinking is the deliberate application of logic and reasoning. It's a 'top down', ego-driven, conscious process where we bring all our experience to a given problem and follow a series of steps to arrive at a considered conclusion. It's the kind of thinking most often taught in schools. It's rational, methodical and depends on the application of existing paradigms. Analytical thinking enables us to plug away at puzzling problems and solve them over time.

Spontaneous thinking is a non-linear, 'bottom up' process, which takes place independently of conscious thought. It's unpredictable, apparently random and a little mysterious. It's the kind of thinking that enables us to outwit the algorithms of computers, to find answers to riddles, to combine previously independent concepts and to arrive at brilliant insights. When it comes to artistic epiphanies, this is where the magic happens. Whereas analytical thinking is linear, spontaneous thinking works in parallel and has vastly more processing power. It is spontaneous thinking that we rely on for creative inspiration – and to banish the Demon of the Blank Page.

The mode of thinking that you employ depends – and I hope you'll indulge me with just a little more neuroscience here – on what your prefrontal cortex is up to.

The prefrontal cortex is the executive centre of the brain. When we're consciously thinking, our prefrontal cortex is hard at work. Paradigms are recalled, decisions are taken and reason is king. The prefrontal cortex loves analytical thinking. It's great at evaluation. If it were a teacher, it would probably love marking. We need the prefrontal cortex to help us decide whether our ideas are any good, but it's unlikely to come up with moments of genius itself.

The problem is that as soon as the Demon of the Blank Page comes knocking and the vast imaginative void yawns before us, our first instinct is to double down on effort, to concentrate and think harder, to activate our prefrontal cortex.

And it's the worst thing we can do.

By bringing the full force of our conscious, rational minds to bear on the problem, we're reducing our capacity for spontaneous thought. Despite our best intentions, we're actually limiting the processing power of our brains and making an innovative solution less likely.

Dating from the late 15th century, *The Last Supper* by Leonardo da Vinci is considered one of the greatest narrative paintings of all time. A masterclass in perspective, gesture and character, it depicts the moment Jesus tells his apostles that one of them will betray him.

Despite the accomplishment of the final work, we know from accounts of Leonardo's life that the painting did not come easily. Each morning the artist would arrive at the church and monastery of Santa Maria delle Grazie in Milan and contemplate the wall on which he had been commissioned to paint. Then he would wander among the flowers and trees of the church gardens, often without having lifted a brush. After this had been going on for some time, the watchful church prior reported Leonardo's dereliction of duty to the Duke of Milan, the patron of the project. The duke summoned Leonardo to his castle and asked him what the hell was going on. He'd commissioned a highly regarded artist to paint a wall at great expense and the wall remained... unpainted.

Leonardo replied crisply, 'Men of lofty genius sometimes accomplish the most when they work the least.' The duke was temporarily silenced, so Leonardo added that one of the problems preoccupying him was the face of Judas, but now he thought that the prior would make an excellent model.

Leonardo understood something many of our greatest artists, thinkers and scientists have themselves discovered to be true: if you seek inspiration, you have to take time to step away from the blank page. After all, the word inspiration literally means to breathe in, to take a deep breath, to chill out. When we're tense or anxious or fearful, our brain shuts down all but the essential functions we need to fight or take flight.

As soon as we stop actively hunting for inspiration, our neurological orientation shifts from the limited processing power of rational thought to the far more profound, insightful and powerful operation of our unconscious neural network. This is why those 'aha' moments often happen when you're in the shower or washing the dishes or when you've just woken up. Or why, when you're struggling to remember someone's name, it comes to you only after you've stopped trying to recall it.

Now, please note: I'm not suggesting that the Demon of the Blank Page showing up is an excuse for you to lose yourself in Netflix. The kind of diversionary activity you undertake needs to be serene enough to allow your unconscious mind the space to do its thing.

When Einstein was stuck with an intractable mathematical challenge, he would put down his pen and pick up his violin. Me, I like to go for a run in the hills of south Wales, where I live. For many people, a short walk is all it takes. As Margaret Atwood has observed, 'Slow walking leads to rumination, which leads to poetry'. Indeed, if you do step outside, you'll probably find that the Demon of the Blank Page is unlikely to come with you. A 2014 study by researchers at Stanford University, California, found that your capacity for creative thought improves by up to 60% when you're walking rather than sitting. Meditation can help too: mindfulness exercises have been shown to aid creativity by encouraging the freer association of random ideas.

Unfortunately, our 'always on' digital lives don't allow much room for daydreaming and the fallowness of boredom. Our phones are never far away. Our brains fizz with blasts of dopamine as we hunt down likes, and flinch with shots of cortisol as

we encounter yet another infuriating news story. Making space and time for the ideas to find you is one of the most important things you can do if you seek inspiration.

Another strategy to help you defeat this particular demon is to get out of your own way. Most of us, understandably, think of ourselves and the grey matter between our ears as the source of our ideas. When the ideas aren't coming, we blame ourselves, we become stressed. And the more stressed we become, the less likely the ideas are to arrive.

But what if we shift the emphasis? From having ideas to receiving them.

This is how the Greeks thought about creativity. If you were a poet or an artist or a musician in ancient Greece, you believed that your ideas came not from within, but from the Muses, the nine daughters of Zeus. Your focus was not on squeezing another creation from your addled mind but simply getting yourself into the right kind of relaxed mood for the Muses to pay you a visit.

This belief that the ideas are already out there, somewhere beyond the self, is still very common today among the most creative human beings on the planet. For David Lynch, the artist and filmmaker renowned for his dark and dreamlike imagination, ideas are like fish: 'You don't make the fish, you catch the fish. Trillions and zillions of ideas, and they're all there, just waiting to be caught.' Phoebe Waller-Bridge, the creator of the award-winning TV shows *Fleabag* and *Killing Eve*, once said in an interview, 'I always feel as though the story is there, floating around in my peripheral vision. I just need to catch sight of it for a second.' And according to legendary record producer Rick Rubin, 'Ideas don't come from out of the blue and they don't come merely from us. We're tuning into them, overhearing them, remembering them and recognizing them.'

This kind of approach removes the conscious, ego-driven self from the equation and, as we now know from our brief lesson in neuroscience, deactivates the prefrontal cortex, initiating spontaneous thinking.

The artist, producer, composer, writer and thinker Brian Eno is surely one of the most creative people of our age, so it's heartening to know that even he bumps up against the Demon of the Blank Page now and again, and finds himself bereft of ideas. He describes the experience in his diary as being on 'the edge of the abyss'.

When he faces this unwelcome void, he leaves his studio and – even if a deadline is looming – does something counterintuitive: he hurls himself into that abyss. He stops hunting for inspiration, and the moment he gives up the battle and cedes control is usually when his fortunes change. He writes, 'At the point of giving up I'm suddenly alive again.' Slowly, inexorably, the ideas return, but only once he's stopped looking for them.

Just for the sake of argument, let's say you've taken the time to step away from the blank page. You've switched off your phone, gone for a walk, meditated. You've relocated the source of your ideas from inside your own head to somewhere out in the ether. You've dimmed your prefrontal cortex and enabled spontaneous thinking. You've even cast yourself into the abyss à la Eno. What if, after all this, the Demon of the Blank Page is still resolutely refusing to budge?

Well, there's one final stratagem you can employ to outwit him: start a different project.

Now, I know what you're thinking: why on earth would I want to embark on yet another creative endeavour when this one is already giving me so much heartache? And you're right. If you begin another project along the same lines as the one being barricaded by the Demon of the Blank Page, then, yes, it may well hit the skids. But if you try something free of whatever strictures you're currently working to, you may surprise yourself.

André Aciman is the celebrated author of *Call Me by Your Name*, a globally successful novel that became an Oscar-winning film. That Aciman came to write his most acclaimed work was purely by accident. He was on a deadline to deliver a different novel. It was ambitious and challenging, and the going was slow. One morning, just before breakfast, he found himself scribbling a few sentences in his journal about a house in Italy overlooking the sea. It was, he said to himself, no more than a diversion before the real work began. Yet after breakfast he found himself returning to his journal.

Because Aciman thought no one would ever read what he was writing, he was liberated from the ponderous self-editing that had been weighing him down on his commissioned novel. He was having fun. The sentences became paragraphs, and the paragraphs pages, and one of the most loved novels of recent years was born.

Having an enjoyable, no pressure 'B' project, the kind of thing you can do for a short time each day, free of the burdensome expectations of your 'A' project, is a great way to keep working in spite of the machinations of the Demon of the Blank Page. Over time, you may even find that the hierarchy flips.

You never know when this particular demon will appear in your path, like an obstinate border guard between you and your imagination. No creative person is ever truly free of him. God knows, he's struck many times in the writing of this book.

If you battle him, he will only grow stronger. Instead, accept his inevitable presence and know that you can always find a way round him.

Just maybe not the way you were intending to go.

Chapter 3

The
Demon
of

Doubt

Imagine

what YOU

would do

if you were confident,

and then *do it.*

Musa Okwonga

When I was at school, I developed an essay-writing problem. The problem wasn't what you might expect. I was a diligent kid – most of the time – and I wanted to do well. The problem was always the opening sentence. As soon as I'd got those first few words down, I'd pause, read them back and ask myself if there wasn't a better way to begin. And so I'd scrunch up a perfectly adequate introduction and start again on a fresh page. But my second attempt would often seem even more turgid than the first, and onto the floor it would go.

Before long, any early momentum was lost. All I had to show for my labours was a pile of wasted paper, a string of overworked words and an oppressive sense of my own inadequacy. Happy days.

The Demon of Doubt is a watchful, zealous creature. He lurks in the wings, observing you keenly, waiting for you to get under way. As soon as he sees you've mustered the courage to break the deadlock between you and the blank page, he'll leap onto your shoulder, look down at those early words or marks on the canvas and launch into his needling refrain, 'Yes, yes, well done for getting started but is it really any good? Surely you can do better than that?'

Take heed of the Demon of Doubt too soon and he will derail your creative impulse and throw you off course. There is a time for critical evaluation in the process of making, but it is much later than you might think.

One of the most underappreciated artists of the 20th century is Corita Kent. She spent much of her life as Sister Corita at the convent of the Immaculate Heart of Mary in Los Angeles. If you'd visited the convent in the 1960s, you'd likely have found Sister Corita in the art room, absorbed in screen-printing colourful graphic posters with messages of peace and love. If you don't know her work, check it out — it's a long way from what you might expect from a member of an austere religious order. As word of Kent's abilities spread, she became renowned as a teacher, someone with an unfussy and inspirational take on creativity. Her list of ten art department rules hangs in my hallway. They are simple and wise.

Rule number 8 is 'Don't try to create and evaluate at the same time. They're different processes.' What Kent understood intuitively has now been confirmed by neuroscience. Today, we know that imagination and evaluation happen in different regions of the brain. The more you conflate these two processes, the less successful you'll be at both.

Remember our friend the prefrontal cortex, the brain's executive centre from Chapter 2? It is our prefrontal cortex that mobilizes the critical skills we need to evaluate work, to consider weaknesses and to find ways of resolving them. Scientists have discovered that when our prefrontal cortex is 'switched off' (which they achieve by a technique called transcranial direct current stimulation, or, in layperson's terms, blasting electrical pulses at someone's head while they wear something that looks like a shower cap) and we stop assessing quality, we become more creative. Jazz musicians show significantly reduced activity in the prefrontal cortex when they improvise. Our prefrontal cortex is less active when we sleep, which is why our dreams are so rich. And the prefrontal cortex is the last part of our brains to develop in adolescence, which explains why kids' imaginations are so free.

The prefrontal cortex is the Demon of Doubt's proxy inside your brain. To allow yourself to be as creative as you can possibly be, to override the power of the prefrontal cortex, you have to cut a deal with this demon. He's never going to disappear completely, and he will have a legitimate role to play when it comes to evaluation, as we'll see. So you say to him, 'Look, I'm going to let you ask some tough questions about the work, just not yet. For now, please bugger off. I'll let you back into the studio when I'm good and ready.'

Then you can really begin.

Now that Doubt has been exiled from your studio – temporarily at least – you can work with freedom. Be as carefree as you can and embrace risk. Sketch. Scribble. Follow flights of fancy,

wherever they may lead. There's no need to dot the i's and cross the t's. Scruffy is good. Use a tool that allows you to draft rapidly. If you're a designer, forget about expensive design software and pick up a pencil. If you're a writer, don't re-read while you're writing – just write. Create as many different possibilities as you can, and then, when you think you're done, create some more. As the inventor Thomas Edison once said, 'When you have exhausted all possibilities, remember this: you haven't.'

Your first ideas, the ones that come easily, are probably going to be the obvious ones, so keep hunting in the long grass for the most outlandish concepts you can find.

As well as committing yourself to volume, you can also choose to work at a time of day when your prefrontal cortex is suboptimal. Or, in other words, a bit dozy. If you're a morning person, try working at night; if you tend to be sharper later in the day, make an early start. Research has shown that this counterintuitive approach often produces more oblique and interesting ideas.

You'll know that this carefree first phase is going well if you start to lose yourself in your work. It was the psychologist Mihaly Csikszentmihalyi who coined the term 'flow' – that frame of mind we enter when we are utterly absorbed in the task at hand, when time stops and the world falls away. The words tumble onto the page as if you're not there. The painting appears on the canvas. The tune writes itself. You become a conduit for a creative force bigger than you. The neurologist

Oliver Sacks describes this experience in his 2017 book *The River of Consciousness*: 'At such times, when I am writing, thoughts seem to organize themselves in spontaneous succession and clothe themselves instantly in appropriate words. I feel I can bypass or transcend much of my own personality, my neuroses. It is at once not me and the innermost part of me, certainly the best part of me.'

It's been discovered that this glorious state of creative flow, which can only be achieved once the Demon of Doubt has been bundled out of the studio, is one of the few times the six most pleasurable chemicals in our brains are simultaneously released: the neurotransmitters norepinephrine, dopamine, endorphins, serotonin, anandamide and oxytocin surge, which is why being creative and working without fear can feel so damn good (and why we'll return to this feeling in Chapter 8).

Sooner or later you'll arrive at the end of your first draft or your first sketch. It may well be scruffy, derivative, overlong and strewn with errors, but at least it exists, beyond you, as a thing in its own right. Now is the time to open your door to the Demon of Doubt, who is probably moping around outside with a cigarette, waiting hungrily for an opportunity to get back in. But if you allow him to do his nit-picking worst and bombard you with negativity, then the little faith you have in your fragile creative construction may disappear completely, so it's best to admit him on your terms and allow him to ask only three simple questions.

Does your work feel true?

Have you made something that is as honest as can be, without fear of how it may affect people's perception of you? Have you spoken with a voice that is as close to your own as you can muster? And have you presented your truth in a form that is distinctive and original? Whether one can ever be truly original is perhaps a moot point, but someone once said to me that a great piece of work is 'a simple truth told in a surprising way', and I think this is an excellent target to aim for.

Does your work make the most of the particular qualities of your medium?

Though it seems kind of obvious, the way we interact with a painting is different from the way we interact with a novel or an album or a play. Each medium allows the artist to do things that can only be done in that medium, and in ground-breaking work these possibilities are often exploited to the full.

I once heard the Beatles' producer George Martin talking about the recording of *Sgt Pepper's Lonely Hearts Club Band*, which was released in 1967. Up until the time the band went into Abbey Road, the prevailing wisdom had been that your task in the studio was to capture the best version you could of a live performance. But, Martin explained, with the luxury of a near-limitless recording budget and no deadline, they began to use the studio itself as an instrument; to do things with sound that could only be done in that context – overdubbing, varispeed, automatic double-tracking – which is why, of all the Beatles records, *Sgt Pepper* remains perhaps the most influential.

Is every element of your work earning its keep?

We often think of the creative process as an additive one. We're bringing into being something that didn't previously exist. We're creating characters, stories, adding colours and light, giving form. But it should also be a process of subtraction. Every word in a sentence should be enhancing the clarity and impact of that sentence for the reader. Every line in your drawing or mark on your canvas should be making some contribution to the mood or meaning of the whole. If a detail isn't adding, then it's diluting and it's better to lose it. 'Every object conceals another,' as the director Luis Buñuel once said.

In 1945, Pablo Picasso created a suite of eleven lithographs. Each lithograph depicts a bull, and each is an evolution of the one before. The series is an illuminating window into the process of one of the 20th century's greatest visual artists.

The first bull is a pretty good likeness but there's nothing special about it; nothing to distinguish it from countless other bulls in countless other artworks. And so Picasso redraws the bull, makes it less naturalistic, more mythical. Over the next few iterations, he works more like a butcher than an artist, slicing up the form, exploring the bull's anatomy. Towards the end of the series, he removes areas of shading and eradicates all but the most indispensable lines. Finally, triumphantly, in the eleventh lithograph, Picasso presents the simplest image of all — the absolute essence of a bull, rendered in the most concise form possible. A bull that is unequivocally Picasso's.

The more ruthlessly Picasso excises detail, the more distinctive and original his bull becomes. Indeed, it's often in the editing, rather than the composition, that we first find a voice that is undeniably our own.

Like many of the other demons in this book, Doubt has a role to play in helping us make our best work, which is fortunate because he is never likely to leave us entirely. It's up to you to know when to allow him into the studio and when to hold him at bay.

Chapter 4

The
Demon
of
Convention

In the beginner's

are many

but in the

mind there

possibilities,

expert's

there are *few.*

Shunryū Suzuki

What sound does a dog make?

If, like me, English is your first language, then
your answer is probably 'woof-woof'. But if you're
Albanian, you'd say 'ham-ham'; or Balinese, 'kong-
kong'; or Greek, 'ghav-ghav'; or Thai, 'hong-hong';
or Welsh, 'wff-wff'. There are almost as many
different ways for describing the bark of a dog
as there are languages in the world.

And none of them is right.

It may be that you come across the odd pooch who
does indeed 'ghav-ghav' or 'hong-hong', but most
of our canine friends sound quite different from
one another. Yet because we're taught when we're
young that a dog makes a certain sound, according
to the lexicon of our mother tongue, over time that
is how we come to hear it. We no longer hear the
sound of a bark as it actually is.

This isn't only true of barking dogs. The longer
we shuffle along this mortal coil, the more cognitive
baggage we accumulate; the more rigid our
perceptions become and the harder it is to respond
to things as they actually are. We become ever
more susceptible to the wiles of the Demon of
Convention, who would always much rather we
walk the road more travelled than dare to try
something new.

Perhaps more than any other of our demons,
it is Convention who most often stands in the way
between good and great. You can enjoy a perfectly
adequate creative career with the Demon of

Convention ambling along by your side. Knock out half-decent versions of whatever the status quo is in your genre and you'll probably do just fine. But if you were happy doing just fine, living in the land of 'perfectly adequate', you probably wouldn't be reading this book.

Each of us has between our ears the most complex biological instrument on the planet, with almost as many neurons as there are stars in the Milky Way. The brain is an organ with the potential to deliver boundless creativity. So why, when the Demon of Convention sidles up to us, do we so readily don the blinkers he holds in his hands?

There are two reasons, the first neurological, the second social.

The first time we encounter a new experience, we're alive to detail and all our senses are alert. Yet very soon the shock of the new is replaced by the dull thrum of the familiar. When it comes to daily life, this is a helpful attribute. If, with every waking moment, we engaged with the world afresh, as if experiencing it for the first time, it would be extremely difficult to get anything done. Imagine if every time you went to make a coffee you were – like a tripped-out acid casualty – wide-eyed and mesmerized by the steam coming out of the kettle.

So our brains' operating system constantly refreshes, setting those programs we use most often to launch automatically, with little, if any, conscious thought required. The way we usually do things becomes neurologically hardwired; our default setting is autopilot. This is a great way

of making sure we're all set to function within our normal environment with the minimum energy cost, but it can leave us at a loss when it comes to original thinking.

There's a cognitive performance test known as the 'candle problem'. It was first developed by the psychologist Karl Duncker in the mid-20th century, but the test has since been repeated many times by other researchers. Participants are given a candle, a book of matches and a box of drawing pins. They're asked to find a way of attaching the candle to the wall and lighting it, without wax dripping on the floor. Three quarters of people fail this test. They try to pin the candle to the wall or use melted wax as an adhesive. Neither of these approaches works.

The solution is to empty the box of drawing pins and use the pins to attach the box to the wall. The box becomes a shelf. The candle sits on the shelf and can be lit. Because most adults are able to see the box only as a box, a container rather than a potential shelf, they're unable to solve the problem. As Leonard Mlodinow notes in his 2018 book *Elastic*, when the test was repeated with members of an Amazon tribe who were unfamiliar with the intended use of the objects, they fared much better.

The candle problem is an eloquent illustration of how fixed we can become in our thinking and how hard it can be to disrupt the conventions that envelop our imagination over time. An unfortunate corollary of this effect is that the more frozen our thinking becomes, the less we are aware of it.

The second reason the Demon of Convention finds us such a soft touch is that we are social creatures, conditioned to behave as the rest of the pack does. We are viscerally afraid of shame or embarrassment.

In the summer of 1998, thirteen third-year art students at the University of Leeds in northern England were preparing for their end-of-year degree show. They'd each been given a grant to help fund the final act of their artistic education. The money was to cover materials, framing, a catalogue and the cheap white wine that is traditional at art events. A week before the show, the students' tutor Terry Atkinson was alarmed to receive a postcard. It read, 'Sorry we can't make the meeting on Tuesday – we're working hard – see you on the opening night. Lots of love, 3rd years.' The postcard had been sent from the sun-drenched Spanish town of Málaga.

Sure enough, come opening night, Atkinson's fears were confirmed. The venue was empty but for a jug of sangria and a stereo playing flamenco. The students' parents, friends and tutors were bussed to a local airport where they looked on, open-mouthed, as the tanned and high-spirited third years tumbled out, having apparently spent their degree-show money on a holiday.

Although the students had, technically, done nothing illegal – they claimed the holiday itself was the artwork – this didn't stop their story convulsing the country in a paroxysm of pious indignation. Condemnation rained down upon the 'Leeds 13' and they went into hiding. 'Con Artists' Spanish Rip-Off' was just one of the many newspaper headlines to roar disapproval.

There was a delicious twist to the story a few days later, when this small group of undergraduates, having sparked a nationwide conversation on what is and isn't a work of art, revealed that the whole thing had been a hoax. They hadn't been to Spain. The postmark on their tutor's card had been forged. The photos of them frolicking in the sunshine, gorged on by the media, had been taken on a Yorkshire beach, and their suntans had been acquired on a borrowed sunbed. Not a penny of the grant had been spent.

And so in a gesture that appeared to defy the conventions of what we understand to be a work of art, they illustrated just how wedded society is to those conventions, and how spiteful it can become when it feels they are threatened.

Given this double whammy of having a brain that would rather take the easy path and do things the way we've always done them, and living in a society that regards rule breakers as dangerous outlaws to be shunned, how on earth are we to cast off the shackles wrought by the Demon of Convention?

An important first step is to acknowledge the bias we have towards conventional problem-solving strategies. When it comes to creativity, a good example is our inclination towards solutions that are additive. A research paper published in *Nature* in 2021 explores this phenomenon: when people are faced with a problem, they tend to solve it by adding new elements rather than taking existing components away, even when the latter is quicker, simpler and more effective. In one test 91 participants were asked to make a pattern symmetrical by either adding or removing coloured boxes. Only 18 people used subtraction. The problem with this human tendency to add, rather than subtract, is that it can lead to clumsy, overworked ideas. When you learned to ride a bike it was probably by your parents adding training wheels or stabilizers; it's been the same for generations. Great to get you going, but not so good once those extra wheels come off. These days kids learn to ride without even being aware they're learning by riding balance bikes: bikes with the pedals removed.

Our sheep-like tendency to follow well-worn paths is often exacerbated by education. At school we learn facts and formulae, we're taught that there is a right way of doing things and a wrong way, even if both give the same answer. Following established patterns is encouraged over experimentation, which perhaps explains why children's performance in creativity tests tends to drop as they get older. It's no coincidence that some of our greatest innovators are autodidacts. If, heaven forbid, Silicon Valley ever had its own Mount Rushmore, Steve Jobs, Bill Gates and Mark Zuckerberg would be the faces carved in stone. All of them were college dropouts.

Being able to escape conceptual mores isn't just a good way to produce innovative creative work, it's an evolutionary necessity. There's a fascinating theory about why there are so many instances of animals apparently seeking intoxication – not just the well-documented cases of elephants or birds becoming drunk on fermented fruit, or cats getting whacked out on catnip, but also wallabies munching poppies, birds chewing marijuana seeds and even dolphins getting high on the emissions from a panicked pufferfish. According to the theory, animals often become stuck in behavioural ruts, and if their environmental circumstances change they become vulnerable. Imbibing narcotics encourages them to 'depattern', to push beyond the boundaries of established

behaviour and to make discoveries – of, say, a new food source or mating ground – which could in time have an evolutionary benefit for the species as a whole.

In a similar vein, microdosing hallucinogens has become à la mode for tech executives looking to enhance their creative thinking. The principle of microdosing is to take just enough LSD or psilocybin to activate the normally dormant neural passageways that facilitate leftfield ideas, but not so much that you find yourself seeing the Godhead in your morning latte. Finding the necessary dosage is a process of trial and error for each individual depending on their physiology, which must make for interesting board meetings now and again.

Of course, taking drugs even in small doses can be dangerous, and it is illegal in most countries in the world, so what other strategies can you employ to free yourself of the manacles of convention, without having to head to the dark web and exchange your hard-won Bitcoins for a vacuum-sealed packet of psychedelics?

One technique is oppositional thinking. Most creative categories come with a set of widely accepted principles that are taken as fundamental to the medium in question. For instance, a work of art is crafted by the hand of the artist, or a novel conforms to the grammatical precepts of the language in which it is written, or music is a series of intentionally produced sounds. Oppositional thinking requires that you first identify these conventions and then see what happens if you do the opposite.

Any paradigm shift requires this kind of thinking. When Marcel Duchamp initiated the era of conceptual art, it wasn't with a work produced in his studio but with a factory-issue urinal signed R. Mutt. Just few years later, in 1922, James Joyce hurled a metaphorical hand grenade into the canon of literature with *Ulysses*, a novel that flaunts pretty much every linguistic rule you can think of. And, in 1952, the composer John Cage forever changed our perception of the parameters of music. He achieved this with a piece that instructed the orchestra *not* to play for 4 minutes and 33 seconds.

In his diary Brian Eno records his friend, the artist Peter Schmidt, talking about 'not doing the things that nobody had ever thought of not doing'. And once you've wrapped your head round this conundrum, it's a great place to start. You can apply the principle to your own particular practice. What are the things you do when you're working that you, or indeed others, always tend to do? And what would happen if you didn't do them?

The Demon of Convention likes nothing more than routine. He's most comfortable with the familiar. To send him packing sometimes you just need to, well, get packing. In Matthew Syed's brilliant book *Rebel Ideas*, he cites a study by the economist Peter Vandor. A group of students were asked to come up with business ideas before and after a term at university. Half of them went to live abroad for the term; the other half stayed at home. The ideas of the former group were rated 17% higher than those of their stay-at-home peers, whose ideas actually declined in quality over the course of the term.

In another experiment, students were given a test of creative word association. Before the test, half were asked to think about living abroad and imagine what life would be like in another country; the other half were asked to think about life in their home town. The former group were judged to be 75% more creative in their responses than the latter.

Travel across borders isn't the only path to original ideas. Travel across genres can be too. Constantly exposing yourself to new work, in fields other than your own, will often lead to an unpredictable and bountiful cross-pollination.

Examine the career of any artist or creative who has successfully stayed at the top of their game for an extended period of time and you'll discover they have their own way of keeping the Demon of Convention at bay. For the musician and performer David Bowie, it was about not becoming comfortable: 'If you feel safe in the area that you're working in, you're not working in the right area. Always go a little further into the water... Go a little out of your depth. And when you don't feel that your feet are quite touching the bottom, you're just about in the right place to do something exciting.' For the artist Chuck Close, it was about 'problem creation' rather than 'problem solving': 'ask yourself an interesting enough question and your attempt to find a tailor-made solution to that question will push you to a place where, pretty soon, you'll find yourself all by your lonesome.'

In recent years there have been anxious discussions among creative communities about the rise of artificial intelligence and the fearful prospect of computers replacing humans in the arts. Code that can write stories, compose music, paint portraits, design logos and develop screenplays has already been written. If you depend upon your creativity for a living, this can be a chilling thought, but it needn't be. Programs like these are reliant on being fed thousands of examples of a given genre, from which they identify patterns. Using these patterns or algorithms, they create their own versions. However, this kind of 'creativity' is by definition derivative. A computer can only ever emulate what has gone before; it cannot break new ground. A computer is bound by the Demon of Convention in everything it does.

You, on the other hand, are not.

The
Demon
of
Constraints

Every wall

is a gate.

Ralph Waldo Emerson

I'm writing this book – or at least attempting to write this book – in the midst of a pandemic. Anxiety hangs in the air like static electricity. When they're not lost in digital narcosis, my locked-down kids demand constant attention. The minute I step away from my desk, which is beside a staircase on a main family thoroughfare, the cat, with vindictive malevolence, delights in leaping onto it and scattering my papers. The wall in front of me is tiled with hopeful yellow Post-it notes, scribbled with headline topics, yet the words on them resolutely refuse to mutate into compelling prose.

And so I daydream.

I daydream of a retreat high in the mountains with a silent study where I sit alone in spectacular seclusion. Opposite my vintage Scandinavian desk are floor-to-ceiling windows, which look out onto a profoundly inspiring vista. Let's make them French windows opening onto a balcony where I can reflect contentedly after a fruitful and fulfilling morning's work. There is no cat. There are no children. My only companion is a sage Buddhist monk to guide me on my creative journey. He also makes an excellent martini.

Would this book be any better, or any easier to write, if my imagined idyll were to become a reality? It's impossible to say – my advance just about covered a new set of pencils! But the research that's been done into how we perform creatively with and without limitations would suggest that I'd find it just as tough, if not tougher, up there in the mountains.

The Demon of Constraints will almost always conjure up some kind of obstacle that we have to leap over, sidestep or break through in order to reach our objective. He is perhaps the most inventive, the most creative, of our mob of mischief-making miscreants. But – and here's the weird thing – he can also turn out to be the most helpful. On those almost-never occasions when we find ourselves working without restrictions, when we have an open brief, an open mind, time, money, and all the materials we desire at our fingertips, the boundless possibilities can be crippling. If we're able to make work at all, it's likely to be much the same as what we've done before: there's nothing to challenge us to think or act differently, so we defer to whatever it is that we normally do. Yet if the Demon of Constraints is too enthusiastic and hurls too many obstacles in our path, then he can, of course, thwart us completely.

If we are to dance with this demon, how do we make sure he doesn't crush our toes?

Well, the first thing to say is that there are two kinds of limitation one is likely to encounter on any creative journey: the imagined and the real. As we've already seen, even when we're feeling at our least inspired, we're still able to be incredibly creative with the reasons why it's impossible for us to work. We can think up all kinds of abstract impedimenta to stop us getting on with the act of making. Ridding ourselves of these fanciful mental millstones is the business of other chapters. Actual, real-world constraints require a different approach.

There are two stories I'd like to share with you which illustrate that, no matter how grave the encumbrance tossed in your path by the Demon of Constraints, there is always a way around.

Chris Wilson is a British-born artist who spent much of his life in America. A childhood blighted by dysfunctional relationships and abuse led Wilson to heroin and crack cocaine, which in turn led to jailtime. On one of his stretches inside, Wilson got clean. Finally free of the narcotic fog that had held him in stasis for so long, Wilson felt an irresistible urge to express himself visually – to paint.

Unfortunately they're not big on art classes in San Quentin State Prison, so Wilson was often stymied in his attempts to get hold of materials: paper was fairly easy to come by, but paint and brushes, not so much. With an improvisatory brilliance born of a junkie life lived on the on the margins, Wilson found a way round this impasse – he discovered that you can paint with Skittles. Four or five Skittles of the same colour, crushed up and mixed with a little water and toothpaste make a pretty passable ink.

Heat up the tip of a plastic knife from the canteen, fold in a lock of your own hair and you have a brush. Before long, Chris Wilson became better known as the Prison Da Vinci (there's a film about him online with the same title). Today he's back in the UK and makes a living as an artist.

There's also the hugely impressive and inspiring tale of Guilhem Gallart. To French hip-hop fans Gallart is better known as 'Pone', the producer of some of the biggest-selling rap recordings in France in the 1990s. In 2015, after a run of unaccountable illnesses, Gallart was diagnosed with amyotrophic lateral sclerosis, better known as ALS, a form of motor neurone disease.

It's a devastating diagnosis to receive. ALS is incurable and progressive, slowly stealing physical attributes until the sufferer is unable to move or speak. For some people, the disease becomes too much and they give up. But not Gallart. Despite now being tetraplegic, fed through a tube and kept alive with a ventilator, able only to blink, he is as creative as he has ever been. As well as writing a blog for fellow sufferers and their families, in 2019 Gallart completed an album inspired by the work of Kate Bush, which she subsequently endorsed, and at the time of writing he is working on a children's book. His music and writing are both executed by the same painstaking method: note by note and letter by letter, using eye-tracking software.

For most of us, the obstacles placed in our paths by the Demon of Constraints are unlikely to be as challenging as those faced by Wilson and Gallart. Few of us will be unfortunate enough to experience incarceration, be it in jail or within our own bodies. Yet there will, without question, still be obstacles of one kind or another.

And could it be that these obstacles end up making our work better than it would otherwise have been?

There are the well-known stories, like the one about Beethoven's deafness enabling him to transcend the compositional conventions of his time in his much-lauded and more experimental later work. Or the story of how Matisse came to produce his famous cut-outs because he was unable to stand at the easel after cancer surgery.

But there are lesser-known tales too.

One of the greatest – and bestselling – children's books of all time is *Where the Wild Things Are* by Maurice Sendak. Few of those who love the story of Max and the wild things, with their terrible teeth and terrible roars and terrible eyes and terrible claws, know that the book began life as *Where the Wild Horses Are*. Sendak's editor Ursula Nordstrom was, however, unimpressed with Sendak's illustrations of horses. As she leafed through the first mock-up, she asked disparagingly, 'Maurice, what *can* you draw?' Sendak replied, 'Things!' And, as it turned out, he could, brilliantly.

There's an incredible music video for a track called *Hibi No Neiro* by the Japanese indie band Sour. You can check it out on YouTube. Eighty fans of the band were filmed remotely via webcam performing a series of choreographed and precisely timed-out movements. These individual shots were edited together over many weeks and months to create a mesmerizing tapestry of coordinated movement. It's undoubtedly one of the most inventive videos of all time. It has won countless awards and been included in the permanent collections of a number of museums. But it came about because of – rather than in spite of – the challenges that the creative team faced.

The band were at home in Japan while the director and creative team were thousands of miles away in New York, wondering how on earth they would make a video given the paltry production budget and geographical limitations. According to Hal Kirkland, the creative director, the idea came when 'we stopped identifying what we didn't have and started thinking about what we could do with what we did.'

Herein lies the secret of overcoming the Demon of Constraints. It's a psychological exercise of reframing: instead of seeing absence, you look for opportunity.

I can think of few better illustrations of this than the work of photographer Jacqui Kenny. I first came across Kenny's landscape photography on Instagram. Her images display a vast array of locations around the world: from Senegal to Chile, Mongolia to the USA. They are poetic, quiet, wistful. The palette is muted, often pastel shades; there are rarely people in the photographs, which lends an extra stillness, and the camera used has a very wide lens, usually capturing scenes beside a road. These qualities alone were enough to motivate me to hit the follow button.

Once I did, I discovered something incredible: Kenny 'took' the photographs without ever leaving home. Her handle on Instagram is The Agoraphobic Traveller and for good reason. Despite enjoying photography and travel, Kenny experiences the anxiety disorder agoraphobia, which makes it hard for her to leave her London apartment. So she has taken to exploring the world via Google Street View. When she encounters a scene that arrests her photographer's eye, she simply takes a screen grab. Her account has over 130,000 followers and her work has been shown all over the world. Kenny explains, 'You don't have to let your limitations stop you achieving your goals. They don't define you. Sometimes you can make them work for you.'

A central tenet of the Japanese martial art of Aikido is that when you stop resisting something you remove its power over you. The more we rail against our lack of time or money or materials, the bigger a barrier they become. The sooner we accept them for what they are, the quicker we'll find a way round them. And counterintuitive though it may seem, researchers have proven that the more constraints we face, the more creative we become. In one experiment, college students were tasked to come up with a new invention. Some were restricted to an arbitrary set of parts, such as a hook, a sphere and a ring; others to a category like furniture, appliances or toys; a third group were limited to a given set of parts and a specific category. The inventions of the students who could choose neither the parts nor the category proved to be way more imaginative and original than the inventions of the students who could choose one or both.

Booker Prize-winning author George Saunders teaches a writing class at Syracuse University in New York State. One of his favourite exercises to push his students into new creative territory is to ask them to write a story in 45 minutes. The story has to be exactly 200 words, no more, no less, and the students can use only 50 different words. The results are stories that are livelier, more dramatic and – paradoxically – more distinctive than those normally produced by the class. Saunders isn't entirely sure why it works so well, but he thinks it's to do with the constraint jolting the students out of their complacency, disrupting the idea they have in their heads of the kind of writer they are, and challenging them to find new ways to express themselves.

And so the Demon of Constraints becomes an ally rather than an enemy. Explore the process of the greats in your own medium and you'll notice that, over time, many of them will have sought to do 'more and more with less and less' – to paraphrase the artist Marina Abramović's brilliant description of the creative process. They push themselves further by creating more restrictive constraints. And the more they limit themselves, the stronger their voice becomes.

You can try this yourself. Think about your own creative toolbox and your favourite tool. If you're a painter, what's the colour you most like to use?

If you're a writer, what person do you normally write in? If you compose songs, what's your favourite chord? Now paint without that colour, write in a different person or compose without using that chord.

A world without the Demon of Constraints is a fantasy land; it's a world of impossible hilltop writing retreats and cocktail-making monks. This demon exists, and he's going to come knocking on your door. Don't try to keep him out. Invite him in and let him take you and your work to a place you wouldn't have got to on your own.

Chapter 6

The
Demon
of
Criticism

To avoid criticism,

do

say

and # be

nothing,

nothing,

nothing.

Elbert Hubbard

One of my favourite observations about making art comes from Philip Guston. He once said, 'When you're in the studio painting, there are a lot of people in there with you – your teachers, friends, painters from history, critics... and one by one if you're really painting, they walk out. And if you're really painting YOU walk out.' It's an elegant description of how you know creative work is going well when the outside world falls away and you lose yourself in the process. But there's a catch in Guston's sage observation that is left unsaid: sooner or later you're going to have to let all these people back in.

There are few writers, composers or artists who make work solely for themselves. We create to express ourselves, and the act of expression is only completely fulfilled when that expression has been heard. And you can be sure, once your novel has been written, your song recorded or your painting hung, that the Demon of Criticism, like a modern demagogue with a loud-hailer, will do all he can to drum up the competing voices of your audience into a cacophony. Every member of that audience is likely to have an opinion. While some of them will, hopefully, love what you've done, others may well hate it. Through a pernicious sleight of hand the Demon of Criticism is somehow able to make us forget the words of the former, while the stinging remarks of the latter go straight to the heart.

In today's world of Instagram, Twitter, Facebook and YouTube, opinions come fast and easy. Barbs are hurled through cyberspace with lethal precision,

often from beneath a cover of anonymity. Amid this deluge of opinion, it can be tough to hear anything clearly. One way to make sense of the din is to imagine three concentric circles. In the first circle, at the centre, is you. In the second circle are people you know personally and respect – your friends and peers. In the third is everyone else, the armchair critics of cyberspace and their professional counterparts. The weight you afford any opinion should – in, erm, my opinion – depend on where it originates relative to the centre: the closer to the centre, the greater its worth.

Let's start at the periphery, in the third circle, with the tastemakers, the gatekeepers, the critics and the wider world.

On 6 June 1956, a young singer from Memphis called Elvis Presley was reviewed in the *New York Times* by the critic Jack Gould: 'Mr Presley has no discernible singing ability. His specialty is rhythm songs which he renders in an undistinguished whine; his phrasing, if it can be called that, consists of the

stereotyped variations that go with a beginner's
aria in a bathroom. For the ear, he is an unutterable
bore.' Ouch. Even though this is one of the most
egregious critical missteps ever, it's maybe wrong
to single out Mr Gould, as there are countless other
examples of celebrated critics making terrible calls.
This is due to the inherently conservative nature
of cultural criticism, as well as the fact that a
bad review is much more fun to read – and write
– than a good one. Critics evaluate new work in
the context of what already exists, and anything
that strays too far from what they know and feel
comfortable with is likely to be shot down.

This timid traditionalism is magnified out there in
cyberspace. Imagine the tirade of sanctimonious
indignation that would have seeped into the
comments box had Mark Rothko been able to post
his colour field paintings on Facebook, or Bridget
Riley her Op Art on Twitter.

What then of the gatekeepers? The publishers, editors, gallerists, label bosses, those whose job it is to seek out great work. Well, they don't fare much better.

If you're one of the hundreds of millions of people to have enjoyed the many books of Theo Geisel, it may surprise you that Dr Seuss, as he's better known, almost gave up on his writing career before it had properly begun. Having been rejected by a publisher for the twenty-seventh time, he was storming home to burn his manuscript and be done with the whole business of books. By chance he bumped into a friend – a friend who had just been given a job in publishing. He talked Theo into giving it one last try. According to the now adored writer, 'If I'd been going down the other side of Madison Avenue, I'd be in the dry-cleaning business today.' When Fred Astaire made his first screen test for MGM, his performance was annihilated in just ten words: 'Can't act. Can't sing. Slightly bald. Can dance a little.' Record label Decca passed on the Beatles because 'guitar groups are on their way out'. And Joanne Rowling, who has sold half a billion books, was rejected by twelve publishers before Bloomsbury took a punt. They gave her an advance of just £1,500 and advised her to change her writing name to 'J.K.', fearing young boys wouldn't want to read a book about a wizard written by a woman.

The world would be immeasurably poorer without the Lorax, Sgt Pepper or Harry Potter, and so it's alarming to know how much we owe to the persistence of their creators, and how little to the gatekeepers of culture.

Yet even when those gatekeepers call it right and identify a work that deserves a wider audience, sometimes that wider audience is not ready. Herman Melville's *Moby Dick* has sold over 25 million copies. Most fans of literature have either read it or, like me, have it on their one-day-I-really-must-get-round-to-reading-it list. Yet when Melville died in 1891, some forty years after the publication of his magnum opus, only 3,715 people had bought a copy of the epic tale of the whale.

The Demon of Criticism would have you believe that commercial and critical success is an absolute reflection of your talent and achievement. He wants you to think that without it you've failed. But the road to acclaim is, in the words of those lads from Liverpool rejected by Decca, a long and winding one. There are plenty of places to get lost along the way. To arrive there isn't just about talent, it's also about luck. As the Beatles, Elvis, J.K. Rowling, Dr Seuss and the rest would be able to tell you, a rejection today does not mean there will be no success tomorrow. Nor does a lifetime of rejection mean your work is without merit, as Van Gogh – who is said to have sold only one painting during his life – might add.

Let's move a little closer to the centre of our circle.

What of our friends and peers? What are their opinions worth?

As you've probably gathered by now, this book is all about how arduous any creative journey is likely to be. Having people — or even just one person — around to dry your tears, make you a cup of tea with an extra sugar when you really need it and, most importantly, piece together your shattered ego when it lies in bits on the floor is a wonderful thing. But your lover and your friends can never be entirely trusted sources of evaluation. It's not their job. They'll always err towards the upbeat, the positive and the encouraging. And if they don't, they probably won't end up being friends or lovers for long.

With your peers, those makers who travel the same path, it's different. Having a close critical relationship with someone who 'gets it' can be helpful in encouraging you to push forward and challenge your complacency. This is why there have been so many close artistic friendships: Andy Warhol and Jean-Michel Basquiat; Truman Capote and Harper Lee; James Baldwin and Toni Morrison; Francis Bacon and Lucian Freud; Helen Frankenthaler and Grace Hartigan. Yet these relationships are laced with ego. At any given point one party will be enjoying more success than the other, which makes it impossible for an opinion to be given without some kind of bias creeping in.

The ideal is to find someone who sits between these two camps. Someone who loves you *and* understands your medium; someone who isn't afraid to tell it like it is. Someone like Alma Reville.

Alma Reville was a screenwriter and editor in Hollywood. She was also the wife of Alfred Hitchcock. When Hitch had completed the first cut on his masterpiece *Psycho*, he showed it to a small circle of confidants. They loved it. Buoyed by their adulation, Hitch took the film home to show Reville. As the final reel spooled to an end, the great director turned expectantly to his wife. She shook her head and said, 'You can't let it go out like that.' One can imagine the look of bafflement appearing in those small, dark eyes set above lugubrious jowls. Reville had noticed something that no one else had, or perhaps something no one had dared to point out to the maestro: after Janet Leigh had been murdered in the shower, her corpse was still visibly breathing.

When Hitchcock received a lifetime achievement award from the American Film Institute in 1979, a year before his death, he gave special thanks to 'four people who have given me the most affection, appreciation and encouragement, and constant collaboration. The first of the four is a film editor, the second is a scriptwriter, the third is the mother of my daughter, Pat, and the fourth is as fine a cook as ever performed miracles in a domestic kitchen. And their names are Alma Reville.'

Hitchcock owed an extraordinary amount to his wife. Had it not been for the vehement sexism of the day, Reville would no doubt have been a celebrated director in her own right. Hitch was lucky to have her. Even if you don't have the good fortune to find your own Alma, there are probably still friends and peers you can turn to for opinions on your work. Just remember that these opinions come filtered through ego or love or rivalry or concern and can only ever be opinions, not fact.

It's worth acknowledging here, too, that sometimes just sharing your work with a third party is enough to reveal flaws that you'd previously not noticed. Romy Madley Croft of the British band The xx has described how inviting someone into the recording studio to listen to a track allows her to hear the song anew. The person doesn't have to say anything for Madley Croft to know what's working and what still needs work. Even if someone does identify a problem, it's still worth being wary of their suggested solution. As the writer Neil Gaiman has observed, 'When people tell you something's wrong or doesn't work for them, they are almost always right. When they tell you exactly what they think is wrong and how to fix it, they are almost always wrong.'

Maybe this is why so many artists and writers deliberately leave a period of days or months before returning to evaluate a completed work. It's a way of seeing it from a distance, of gaining the perspective of a third party without having to actually engage with the bothersome opinions of said third party. Zadie Smith encourages fellow writers to 'try to read your own work as a stranger would read it, or even better, as an enemy would.'

And so, at last, we arrive at the centre of our circle.

At the centre of the circle is you.

You've reached deep inside yourself to examine a truth. You've worked hard to make that truth manifest in the most authentic way you possibly can. You alone have experienced the setbacks, the heartache, the drama, perhaps even the fleeting moments of joy. And ultimately, you alone know in your heart how successful you've been.

All those voices whipped up by the Demon of Criticism are just voices. They can help guide you and encourage you and steel you to stay on course. They can even puff up your artistic ego from time to time. But they can also, if you allow them, gnaw away at your creative soul until you're just a husk.

Listen to them when it suits you. But don't listen too often or too hard.

Chapter 7

The Demon of Theft

Everyone

who you could possibly
steal from at this point
in human evolution

is a
thief.

Jeff Tweedy

If you have an ear for a well-crafted tune from the last forty years – and I'm guessing that includes pretty much everyone reading this book – then there's a good chance that among your favourite songs is at least one that owes its existence to a chance moment more than fifty years ago.

The Winstons were a soul band from Washington, DC. One spring day in 1969, in a recording studio in Atlanta, Georgia, they hit a problem. They'd just laid down the track *Color Him Father*. They were pleased with the single about a boy's love for his stepfather and they were right to be: it would go on to win a Grammy and be their biggest hit. The problem was what to put on the B-side.

Lead singer Richard L. Spencer, aware that his bandmates were short on ideas and ready for a break, proposed they lay down a version of the gospel classic *Amen, Brother*. But the song came up too short, so they added a guitar riff. Still too short. To pad out even more time, drummer Gregory Coleman decided to add a four-bar drum break. GC, as he was known, played the same beat for two bars, delayed the snare in the third, and left the first beat of the fourth bar open, before finishing with a syncopated flourish and an early crash cymbal. Now running at two and a half minutes, *Amen, Brother* was just about long enough to make a credible B-side and the band hurried out of the studio in search of the nearest bar.

Spool forward to New York in the early 1980s. The block parties in Brooklyn, Queens and the Bronx have given birth to hip-hop. The innovation of using two turntables to provide rappers with an infinite loop of beats, together with the widespread availability of the sampler to isolate any part of an existing tune, means that DJs are plundering the back catalogue of soul and funk records for hidden treasures they can repurpose. Clean syncopated drum breaks are particularly sought-after. It turns out that GC's six-second break – 'the Amen Break', as it would become known – is just perfect.

Before long, you can hear it everywhere. Looped, sped up, slowed down, cut up, it becomes the backbeat to a seemingly infinite jukebox of tunes.

Salt-N-Pepa are among the first artists to give the break a new home on *I Desire*. It is the sonic spine to N.W.A.'s explosive *Straight Outta Compton* and countless other hip-hop tracks. Later, you hear it in dance tracks by the Prodigy and house tunes by Carl Cox. It underpins songs by artists as diverse as Amy Winehouse, David Bowie and Oasis. An entire genre of dance music, jungle, is built around those six seconds laid down by GC one fine day in Atlanta. It's impossible to say for sure how many tracks owe a debt to the Amen Break, but at the time of writing, the WhoSampled app has identified more than 5,000.

And so a six-second drum break, conjured out of nowhere to fill time and give a bunch of bored musicians an excuse to get out of the studio, for more than fifteen years a dusty recording footnote, became a cornerstone of music history.

I tell this story not only because the Winstons deserve recognition – incredibly, they're yet to

receive a penny in royalties – but also because
it belies one of the central myths of the creative
process: the notion that ideas can ever truly be
original.

We like to believe, because we're ego-driven, self-
obsessed creatures, that each of us alone is the
sole parent to our ideas. We kid ourselves that
inspiration is ineffable, miraculous, a kind of magic.
The muses smile upon us and – bingo! – out of
nowhere pops an idea. All those influences that
have led us to this point evanesce in a convenient
puff of amnesia.

The truth, of course, is that nothing comes of
nothing.

Our success as a species rests on our ability to
build on, reimagine and advance the ideas of others.
Sir Isaac Newton famously said, 'If I have seen
further it is by standing on the shoulders of giants'
– his point underscored by the fact that he had
borrowed the phrase 'shoulders of giants' from
John of Salisbury, who had himself acquired it from
Bernard of Chartres.

As a species we're neurologically hardwired to
commit creative larceny; it's the reason we've
survived so long. For many years it was believed
that Neanderthals were dull, stupid, brutish
creatures, and therefore it was hardly a surprise
that they died out while we smarter *Homo sapiens*
thrived. After all, the Neanderthals were on the
planet for around 300,000 years and all they had
to show for it were a few bone carvings and a way
of turning stone into axe heads, whereas in our

200,000 years – and counting – we have come up with the microchip, self-driving vehicles, quantum mechanics and... karaoke bars.

So it came as a bit of a shock when scientists discovered in 2018 that the average Neanderthal brain was bigger than the one you're using right now. Given their extra grey matter, how come our large-browed cousins advanced so little before dying out, while we continue to innovate and develop new technologies at an exponential rate?

Compare a Neanderthal brain and a human brain closely and you'll see that, though the former is larger, the cerebellum within it is smaller. The cerebellum is responsible for higher cognitive skills, like language processing and social interaction. As a result, compared to contemporary *Homo sapiens*, it is thought that Neanderthals lived in much smaller, isolated groups and were less

able to communicate and share ideas between themselves. Without the ability to take what others had worked out and build on it, to expand on the discoveries of their peers, Neanderthals would have had to learn everything from scratch, progressing little beyond the most rudimentary of skills. As their environmental conditions changed, they were unable to adapt and some scientists believe that this is the principal reason why they died out. Humans are way better at sneaking a look at what someone else has done and asking, 'How can I take that and make it even better?'

We love the fallacy of the lone genius who illuminates the arts or science with a flash of unbidden brilliance, yet the truth is more prosaic: any innovator is profoundly indebted to all previous innovations up to that point.

There is a wonderful letter written by Mark Twain to his friend and fellow author Helen Keller, when the latter had been accused of plagiarism: 'As if there was much of anything in any human utterance, oral or written, except plagiarism! For substantially all ideas are second-hand, consciously and unconsciously drawn from a million outside sources... It takes a thousand men to invent a telegraph, or a steam engine, or a phonograph, or a photograph, or a telephone, or any other important thing — and the last man gets the credit and we forget the others. He added his little mite — that is all he did.'

Few of our most lauded innovators have been humble or honest enough to admit the inevitability of their discoveries as part of the momentum of human progress. Henry Ford was an exception. The 'genius' credited with inventing mass production conceded that he was simply in the right place at the right moment: 'I invented nothing new. I simply assembled into a car the discoveries of other men behind whom were centuries of work.' Indeed, some of the greatest breakthroughs of humankind, though credited to one person in the history books, were 'discovered' simultaneously in different parts of the world – photography, calculus and the theory of evolution being just a few examples.

The notion that any idea depends upon the ideas that have gone before it – let's call it the origin theory of ideas – may not be as magical or romantic as the Virgin birth theory, but it is reassuring. Once we understand that the more we immerse ourselves in the great works of others, the more likely we are to be able to reconfigure them – to 'assemble' them, in the words of Ford – and produce great work ourselves, the less daunting the process of innovation seems.

Tucked away in the darkest corners of YouTube is a clip of Steve Jobs admitting to being 'shameless about stealing great ideas'. That the clip has not been seized upon by the lawyers of Samsung or Google is down to the kind of theft he describes. He talks about stealing ideas for the Macintosh computer from music, poetry, art, zoology and history. It was only by drawing on the findings of a vast array of subjects beyond computer science that Jobs and his team were able to lead a revolution in computing.

Now, I know what you're thinking.

If any creative act depends upon reworking existing ideas, do we really need to worry about the Demon of Theft, who as you may have noticed has yet to put in an appearance by name in this chapter. Is he even a demon at all?

Well, that all depends on how you steal.

If you simply take someone else's work and pass it off as your own, then this is indeed the worst kind of creative theft. Allow yourself to commit larceny of this order and your creative soul will shrivel and your muse will die. You'll also probably end up living in a tent, having been forced to sell your home to pay the legal fees amassed by a high-profile plagiarism lawsuit.

Steal only ideas from within your own genre and this is a kind of cannibalism. And, as I hope I don't need to point out, cannibalism never ends well.

If, on the other hand, you take an element of an existing idea and you transform it, perhaps move it from one medium to another, introduce a new element born of your own personality and experience and take it somewhere new, then no creative crime has been committed.

The singer Nick Cave was once challenged about a song that he had written, which shared melodic similarities with a song by someone else. His defence was that rock and roll is 'a feeding frenzy of borrowed ideas' and simply couldn't survive without people 'grabbing stuff from everybody else, all the time'. For him, the only mandate was to advance the stolen idea in some way. You'd know when your theft was successful because someone would then, in turn, steal the idea from you.

When we're young, we fall in love with a medium – painting, music, poetry, dance – and sooner or later we're moved by the impulse to express ourselves in that medium. Inevitably, when we do, we end up imitating those we admire. We can't help it. Sometimes that imitation is conscious, sometimes not. But through imitation we learn. It's how we come to understand the rules of the genre – rules that one day we may have the courage to break. Then there comes a critical point when you no longer copy, you steal: you take existing ideas and – this is the important bit – you make them your own. You give them a quality that comes entirely from you. You rework ideas through your own experience and you speak them in your own voice. Through theft, you become an artist in your own right.

To create is to steal: to steal not only from the worlds of music and sculpture, painting and poetry, cinema and dance, but also from snatched fragments of bus-stop conversations, from old album covers, from graffiti, from billboards, from burger-van menus, from shop-window displays, from dreams... from who knows where.

There's just one thing always to keep in mind as the Demon of Theft hands you your metaphorical swag bag and encourages you to go prowling. As the film director Jean-Luc Godard once said, 'It's not where you take things from – it's where you take them to.'

Chapter 8

The

Demon

of

Accidents

Nothing

I mean the

charge of me,

is ever planned.

work is in

I'm not in charge of it.

Thank God!

Maggi Hambling

ESTUDIO DE
PICASSO

SOLD:
$62000000

We've all been there. That moment when you've freed yourself from the shackles of self-doubt and broken away from the seductive tug of procrastination and – at last – you're under way, you're creating, this feels good, you're actually making something you're happy with. Transfixed by your painting, you reach across, without looking, to dip your brush into the red paint, and as you carefully apply a stroke to the centre of the canvas, you realize that the pot of red paint was in fact blue. No, not now! It's almost as if the Demon of Accidents was waiting in the wings until all the other demons were out of view before abruptly hurling himself into your path.

The only thing we can predict about the Demon of Accidents is that sooner or later he will turn up and do his damnedest to throw you off course.

So what are you to do when such a moment comes to pass?

Well, there's a surprising secret shared by great creatives in all genres, a secret that seems counterintuitive when one thinks about how much we celebrate their individual accomplishments: they are not wholly responsible for their best work.

If you were to ask a bunch of cinema buffs to name the best opening scene of all time, their discussion would likely be long and circuitous, involve a lot of coffee and fail to arrive at a conclusion. Nonetheless, at some point they would almost certainly find themselves talking about Orson Welles's acclaimed 1958 film noir *Touch of Evil*.

The movie opens with a single tracking shot that is a triumph of filmmaking. Welles begins with a close-up of a ticking time bomb before sweeping through the sultry late-night streets of a Mexican border town. There are dramatic wide shots, mesmerizing camera moves, a huge number of extras, even a herd of goats until – almost three and half minutes later – the first cut, to a huge explosion, just as Charlton Heston kisses Janet Leigh, an ominous harbinger of what is to come.

To watch this scene – and many others – from Welles's movies is to witness the precise and deliberate orchestration of the visual. Lights, camera, sound, performance and editing are all delicately choreographed. As a result, it would be reasonable to conclude that it was meticulous planning and storyboarding that enabled Welles to become one of the greatest directors of all time.

Reasonable, but wrong. In fact, the opposite was the case.

Orson Welles loved the unexpected. His greatest hope on a shoot was not that the Demon of Accidents would stay away from the set, but that he would show up each day, because Welles knew that it was in the events beyond his planning that creative magic was most likely to happen. As the maestro himself put it, 'the greatest things in movies are divine accidents. My definition of a film director is the man who presides over accidents... Everywhere there are beautiful accidents... they're the only things that keep a film from being dead. There's a smell in the air, there's a look, that changes the whole resonance of what you expected.'

Way more important to Welles than the dramatic opening of *Touch of Evil* was a later scene, where the two rival cops in the story meet. The corrupt Hank Quinlan, played by Welles himself, notices a pigeon's nest on a windowsill. He picks up one of the eggs in the nest and it breaks in his hand. In a symbolic gesture, Charlton Heston's clean-cut Captain Vargas offers his handkerchief to wipe up the mess. That the nest was on the windowsill was pure chance. Welles spotted it and this became an important moment in the film.

The notion that any artist is in absolute control of every element of their artwork is a fallacy. I remember watching a documentary about the painter Frank Auerbach in which he demonstrated this. He quickly drew six ducks and attempted to make them all exactly the same. Each one was just a beak, an eye and the outline of a head. Yet despite their simplicity, and the artist's aim of consistency, they all turned out to be subtly different. While I'm no Auerbach, I've had a go at recreating this experiment myself...

Even though I too have tried to draw six identical ducks, each seems to have acquired its own personality. My first duck looks like a simple chap, intent on food. The second seems a little scared. The third looks rather cocksure and maybe a bit stupid. The fourth is sad. The fifth is happy. And the sixth, dopey but lovable.

At the moment of creation there are forces at work beyond the artist. If you struggle against them, you'll find yourself frustrated. But if you surrender to them, if you give yourself up to the process and see where it takes you, then maybe the work will exceed even your own expectations.

You know that feeling when you finish a particularly compelling novel that has enthralled you with its intricately drawn characters, complex narrative,

subtle imagery and linguistic experimentation
– how it seems almost inconceivable that it is
the work of any single human intelligence? Well,
that's because, in a way, it isn't. The writer has
allowed the story to go where it wants to go and
the characters to be who they want to be. Hilary
Mantel, the double Booker Prize-winning author
of the *Wolf Hall* trilogy, puts it like this: 'If you think
of any worthwhile novel... no one is clever enough
to do it... you have to take your hands off and see
what shapes the story forms. You must trust the
process, and that can be difficult, because you
have to quell anxiety; the task is to get out of
your own way.'

In other words, you take your hand off the tiller and
say to the Demon of Accidents, 'OK, wherever you
go, I promise to follow.'

It's a curious thing that the more one is prepared to let go, to 'get out of your own way' to use Mantel's illuminating phrase, the more rewarding and enchanting and pleasurable the whole process becomes. Our English word 'ecstasy' comes from the Greek *ekstasis*, which originally means to stand outside oneself. And as any self-respecting ancient Greek artist or musician would have told you, the muses will only visit once you are, literally, ecstatic. If you can stand outside yourself while you work, subjugate your conscious mind and allow yourself to be carried wherever your creative momentum takes you, then you are on the path to creative ecstasy.

The Spanish dancer Tamara Rojo has described how, throughout her long career, she has been motivated by chasing, like an addict, the rare hit of those performances where she feels herself disappear, completely subsumed by the role. Paradoxically, in this most physical of artforms she experiences the 'almost religious, almost metaphysical experience' of escaping her own body; it's as if she is watching the performance from the outside. When she feels like this she is at the height of her powers, able to induce in the audience whatever emotion she chooses. Rojo says that this has happened just a handful of times in three decades of professional dancing, but when it does, 'there is no other experience like it – it's the best feeling.'

So if this feeling of abandoning ourselves to the work, casting off ego and embracing the whims of the Demon of Accidents feels so good – and has the potential to be so fruitful – how might you induce it more often? What techniques can you employ in your practice to encourage the loss of self?

The British artist Maggi Hambling has spoken of how, as soon as she wakes, in that liminal space between consciousness and sleep, she makes a drawing with an ink dropper. Although she is right-handed, she holds the dropper in her left hand, and she closes her eyes to further surrender control. There's no intended subject; she simply allows her hand to take her wherever it wishes. Then, without further reflection, she has breakfast. The drawings created by this accidental process have inspired some of Hambling's most successful paintings and have sometimes revealed a deeper psychological truth of which she hadn't previously been aware.

The Norwegian author Karl Ove Knausgård has described *My Struggle*, his series of six globally successful autobiographical novels, as 'an exercise in giving up control'. His ideal writing state is when he feels like he is a passive partner in the process, more like a reader following the text than its author. To achieve this Knausgård, like Hambling, gets up early to take advantage of a brain that is still not properly awake. He then chooses a word: 'It could be "apple" or "son" or "tooth", anything,' he explains. 'It's just a starting point – a word, an association – and the restriction is that I write about that. It can't be about anything else. Then I just start, without knowing what it's going to be about. And it's like the text produces itself.' No doubt this approach demands copious editing later on, but it's a brilliantly simple way of inducing the state of flow we explored in Chapter 3.

Above all, the most important strategy you can engage is to be mindful when you make — to be alive to the possibilities of each moment and not so wedded to an intended outcome that you miss one of those rare and accidental moments that could take you somewhere altogether more exciting.

To illustrate, let's take a trip to outer space.

The Apollo 8 mission was the first manned mission to orbit the moon. On Christmas Eve 1968, just after 10:30am Houston time, the crew of Apollo 8 were on their fourth orbit. Three times they'd observed the moon from a perspective that no human being had seen until then — an extraordinary spectacle in itself. But then, on the fourth time around, Mission Commander Frank Borman rotated the spacecraft by a few degrees. As he did so, his fellow astronaut Bill Anders happened to catch sight of something out of his side window that took his breath away: the blue pearl that is our planet, slowly appearing above the barren, grey, lifeless surface of the moon. NASA had given the astronauts a strict schedule of images to capture. This unanticipated view was not one of them. Nevertheless, Anders, aware he was witnessing something wonderful, grabbed his highly modified Hasselblad 500 EL and fired off a few exposures before returning, dutifully, to his allocated tasks.

One of those exposures was to enter history. *Earthrise*, as it became known, radically altered our perception of humanity's standing in the universe. For the first time, we could see how beautiful and how lonely our planet is amid the vast blackness of space. The beginning of the environmental movement has been attributed to this one image.

Yet, if the spacecraft had been on the same rotation as it was during its previous orbits, the astronauts on board would not have witnessed the Earth rising above the moon's horizon. And if Anders had not had the gumption to deviate from NASA's schedule, it would not have been witnessed by the world at large.

As we've come to understand, many of the demons we fear most in the creative process can turn out to be a help rather than a hindrance if we respond to them in the right way. Adhere religiously to your initial vision for a work and the work can never exceed your expectations; it can only fulfil them. But if you leave a little space for the Demon of Accidents to pay a visit, he may take you beyond the boundaries of your own imagination.

And you know what?

Maybe that flash of blue is just what your painting was missing.

The Demon of Failure

Sometimes A Fuck Up

It's the angel

on the shoulder

Isn't Really A Fuck Up

of the devil

on your shoulder.

Darby Hudson

It's summer 2012. The hot Spanish sun is unforgiving as it beats down on the quiet streets of Borja, a medieval town a few hours north-east of Madrid. Cecilia Giménez, an elderly resident, takes shelter from the heat in the church of the Santuario de Misericordia.

As Cecilia sits in quiet contemplation, she's unable to take her eyes off a painting of Christ by the artist Elías García Martínez. The fresco is nearly a century old, and the paint is starting to flake. This upsets Cecilia. The church is a special place for her. It's where she married some sixty years ago, and where she has worshipped ever since. Cecilia knows only too well how bare the church coffers are and how unlikely it is that the painting will be restored.

So she makes a decision – a decision that will change not only her life but life within the ancient town in which she lives.

Cecilia decides that she will restore the painting herself.

It's fair to say that Cecilia's technical ability falls someway short of that of the original artist: the Son of God soon bears a closer resemblance to a startled primate. And it's not long before the town's historical association discovers what she's up to. Outraged, they photograph her work and post it online. Although Cecilia claims that she's not yet finished, it's too late. Within hours, before and after images of the fresco have gone viral.

In the UK, the *Daily Telegraph* leads with the headline 'Elderly woman destroys 19th-century fresco with DIY restoration'. *Le Monde* in France is somewhat more emphatic, 'HOLY SHIT – the restoration of a painting of Christ turns into a massacre'. On the American television show *Saturday Night Live* there's a sketch called 'Potato Jesus' that has the audience weeping with laughter. The internet is alive with memes of 'Monkey Christ'.

One can only imagine the psychological effect of global ridicule on the 81-year-old. A woman who loved art, who loved Jesus and who loved her church – a church that many felt she had now desecrated. Sure enough, she soon went into hiding and, it was reported, lost 17 kg in weight. And so Cecilia Giménez's well-intentioned creative endeavour went spectacularly wrong. It became a calamitous clash with maybe the most destructive creative demon of all: the Demon of Failure.

The power of the Demon of Failure is twofold. It resides not only in the havoc and devastation he can wreak in the lives of those, like Giménez, who are unfortunate enough to encounter him, but also in the hold he can have over us. The mere prospect of a possible encounter with the Demon of Failure can be enough to stop us from embarking on a creative act or, if we do get started, from taking the kind of decision that could transform a work from good to great.

We're taught to fear failure from a very young age. We are rewarded when we get something right, admonished when we get something wrong. Our education is usually binary: there is a right answer and a wrong answer. When the teacher returns our homework, we look eagerly for the green ticks and we flinch from the brutality of the red crosses. This continues into our working lives too: the longer we avoid failure, the higher we can hope to climb up the slippery pole. And so we are pushed into what the writer Kathryn Schulz has called the 'tiny, terrified space of rightness' – an awkward and constricted spot where fearfulness reigns, risk is anathema and the chances of doing anything exceptional are nil.

Yet when it comes to creativity, the biggest failure is the failure to fail.

Remove the possibility of failure and you remove the possibility of true discovery.

If you have the courage to forge into unknown territory, the kind of place where a genuine breakthrough could happen, you have to accept that it's more than likely you'll bump into the Demon of Failure while you're there. We love the idea of the 'eureka moment' – that flash of inspiration bestowed upon the lucky recipient, seemingly out of nowhere – but it is, as we've already seen, a myth.

As the writer Steven Johnson has observed, 'The history of being spectacularly right has a shadow history lurking behind it: a much longer history of being spectacularly wrong, again and again.' Delve into the life and work of anyone who has significantly advanced their medium and you'll find a catalogue of dead ends, missteps and bad calls. It's been said of Albert Einstein that no one made more breakthroughs in the world of physics than him, but equally no one had more failures. Often those we regard as geniuses don't have a better hit rate of good ideas versus bad ones than ordinary people; it's simply that they produce vastly more ideas, increasing the probability that they'll chance upon something great.

So one of the most important factors in determining the likelihood of your future creative success is how you respond when the Demon of Failure – inevitably – punches you in the nose.

Do you allow him to block your way while you retreat, clutching a bloody handkerchief to your battered proboscis? Or do you think, 'Aha, if he's in the neighbourhood, then there's a good chance I'm taking the kind of risks I'll need to hit on something good. It's just going to take a little longer than I expected.' It's this kind of mentality that spurs on some of our greatest innovators. Thomas Edison is celebrated as the inventor of the lightbulb, the phonograph and the carbon transmitter in the telephone. Yet the path to these genuinely useful discoveries was littered with over 100 other patented products long since forgotten, like an electric pen, which was noisy, heavy and required jars of messy, dangerous chemicals to maintain the battery; or a talking doll with a voice that many people said was ghastly.

Computer engineers work hard to eliminate error from their systems. Yet if we do the same as creatives, we doom ourselves to make safe, repetitive and uninteresting work. The space where errors occur is the same space where breakthroughs are made. The trouble is that the longer we practise our creative profession, the more uncomfortable we become with mistakes. We believe that our failures should be less frequent because we know more about our craft and therefore, where possible, we shy away from making them. But this is the path to complacency.

Being right gives us nothing more than the fleeting, self-congratulatory buzz of knowing everything is just as we thought it should be. Being wrong jolts us into a reappraisal of our assumptions; it forces us to question what we took for granted and to seek new answers.

The artist Marina Abramović describes in her memoir how, when she's teaching, she has her students sit at a desk with a thousand pieces of paper and a waste paper basket. They spend several hours every day for three months coming up with ideas. Those they like they keep on the desk; the ones they don't, they put in the trash. When they finally exhaust the pile of paper, they are told to discard the ones on the desk and to work only with those they threw out. According

to their mentor, 'the trash can is a treasure trove of things they're afraid to do.'

Often it is our failures that are more fertile, with more fuel for growth than our successes. Indeed, many of our most significant scientific and technological breakthroughs happened because something didn't go to plan. An important tool for me in the writing of this book is the Post-it note. I've tiled the wall behind my laptop with small, sticky yellow squares. On each of them is scribbled something I need to write about; as I wrestle with structure, they can be easily rearranged. They came about because Dr Spencer Silver, a chemist at 3M, was attempting to invent a super-strong adhesive. Unfortunately, he created a super-weak one instead. It was many years later when a colleague, Art Fry, frustrated at the way his bookmark would slip from his hymn book at choir practice, recalled Silver's weak but reusable adhesive and realized the huge potential in this accidental innovation.

Penicillin, Viagra, microwave ovens, X-rays, pacemakers, crisps, cornflakes and countless other products we take for granted today share a similar origin story to that of the Post-it note. Each of them came into being not as the natural outcome of a predictable and rigorous experimental process, but as an unexpected and, at the time, undesirable outcome. A mistake, in other words. It was only because the person responsible for them refused to be stymied and had the courage to wander down this newly opened and unenvisaged path – to see them not as failures but as opportunities – that they came to have value.

The Demon of Failure only has a hold over us so long as he has a hold over our thinking. There's a great story told by the jazz pianist Herbie Hancock about one balmy summer night in Stuttgart, Germany, when he was on stage with the legendary jazz musician Miles Davis. All was going well. Or at least it was until Hancock played the wrong chord, right in the middle of Davis's solo. He describes how he flinched and put his hands over his ears, no doubt fearful of the response – Davis was an unforgiving taskmaster. But what Davis did next shocked Hancock: 'Miles paused for a second and then he played some notes that made my chord right, it made it correct. Which astounded me – I couldn't believe what I heard.'

It was only later that Hancock truly understood what had happened. Davis hadn't heard the chord as a mistake; for him it was simply an unanticipated moment in the piece that required a response, a response that took the music in a different direction. Hancock adds, 'That taught me a very big lesson about not only music, but about life.'

Failures are like weeds. There's no intrinsic property to a weed that makes it a weed; it's simply a plant that we don't want in the garden. A failure is just an event like any other. What makes it a failure is that we judge it to be so from the limited perspective we have at the time. 'This wasn't a desirable or expected outcome,' we tell ourselves, 'and therefore it must be a failure.'

But what if there's another way of seeing it?

There's an illuminating Buddhist parable about a farmer who has a horse. One day the horse escapes. The farmer's neighbour comes by to commiserate, but the farmer is sanguine: 'Thank you for your concern, but who's to say what's bad or good?'

The next day the horse returns. Not only does it come back, but it does so with six wild horses that it has encountered on the plains. Once again, the neighbour visits, this time to congratulate the farmer on the reversal of fortune. Yet the famer shows little emotion: 'Thank you, but who's to say what's bad or good?'

The following day the farmer's son is trying to tame one of the wild horses. He falls and breaks his leg. The neighbour expresses his sorrow at the accident. The farmer replies simply, 'Who's to say what's bad or good?'

Sure enough, a day later, the army visit the farm looking for able-bodied young men to serve in a war that they seem destined to lose. The farmer's son is spared the draft because of his broken leg. And what had appeared to be a terrible misfortune turns out to be exactly the opposite.

This story could go on and on, but you get the point.

We deceive ourselves if we think we have the capacity to say whether something is a success or a failure at the moment it occurs. Of course we can make a call, based on the available evidence at the time, but if you take the long view the truth can turn out to be quite different.

So what of Cecilia Giménez, whom we left, shrunk with depression and in hiding?

Well, within a few days of her becoming a global laughing stock, something unexpected happened in Borja. Tourists came. And not just a few. Thousands of them, all wanting to see Potato Jesus for themselves. Between August and December 2012, 45,824 people visited the Santuario de Misericordia and almost all of them dropped a few euros in the collection box. Within a short amount of time the coffers of this dilapidated church in a long-forgotten Spanish town were overflowing. The money was enough not only to restore the church, but also to provide ongoing care for impoverished elderly Borja residents. There was just one part of the building the restorers dare not touch: Cecilia Giménez's Monkey Christ.

Next time you find yourself facing down the Demon of Failure, and face him you must if you are to take the kind of risks on which creative breakthroughs depend, square up to him, look him hard in the eye, and ask him one simple question:

Who's to say what's bad or good?

Chapter 10

The Demon of Disappointment

There's only

thing

That is one's own

one

certain.

inadequacy.

Franz Kafka

As we've established by now, making creative work is hard. To complete a painting, a story or a song requires courage, persistence and a staunch determination not to be derailed by the demons who would stand in your way. And so it's not uncommon, as you type your final sentence or step back from the easel, to feel a flush of contentment. You did it! Against the odds you brought something into being that didn't previously exist. Though you're yet to acknowledge it, maybe there's the thrilling feeling somewhere deep inside you that this latest work is pretty special. After all the heartache, self-doubt and creative cul-de-sacs, could audience adulation and critical acclaim be just round the corner?

Is this... the one?

Yet even as you dare to dream of royalty cheques and honorary doctorates and humble, heartfelt acceptance speeches, there is an intruder jemmying open the window to your studio. Come the morning, when you return to your masterpiece, you'll find him squatting on it and giggling at your hubris.

His name is the Demon of Disappointment.

Where yesterday you saw flair and originality, today you see cliché and contrivance. The idea burned so brightly in your mind, yet your execution seems so... lifeless.

Pride evaporates.

Hope is gone.

Bugger.

Unless you enjoy dictator-worthy levels of
narcissism and a complete absence of critical
judgment, then, I'm sorry to say, you will come to
know the Demon of Disappointment. If you're a
working artist, he's sure to be kicking round your
neighbourhood. Between breaking into cars and
stealing handbags and chucking burger wrappers,
he'll always find time to pay you a visit.

Remember John Steinbeck, whom we met in the
first chapter, lost in the agony of writing *The
Grapes of Wrath*? The miserable author lamented,
'If only I could do this book properly it would be
one of the really fine books and a truly American
book... I am assailed with my own ignorance
and inability.' More recently, the British writer
Will Self, on being asked to give advice to aspiring
authors, wrote, 'You know that sickening feeling
of inadequacy and over-exposure you feel when
you look upon your own empurpled prose? Relax
into the awareness that this ghastly sensation will
never, ever leave you, no matter how successful and
publicly lauded you become.' This raises a pressing
question: if the Demon of Disappointment is to be a
familiar companion throughout any creative career,
even a long and distinguished one, how are we to
live with him?

Well, the first thing to know is that this demon,
whose presence we are usually aware of only once
we step back to contemplate a finished work,
often occupies a very particular place: the gap
between idea and execution, between concept
and realization. And the idea rendered by your

hand can never be as lustrous and vital as it was in your head. The poet and musician Kae Tempest describes this gap with characteristic honesty in their book *On Connection*: 'There is no success in writing. There are only better degrees of failure... An idea is a perfect thing. It comes to the writer in a breathless dream. The writer holds this idea in their mind, in their body; everything feeds it... But it will never be right. There is no way that a writer cannot injure that idea as they wrestle with it.'

Before you began work on it, your idea was unbound by the limitations of either your medium or your ability. Then it soared; now, inevitably, it stumbles. But you know what? It may not be much to look at, and you may have injured it as you tore it from your imagination, but at least it exists as a thing. A thing that can be worked on, refined, improved.

That you can see the gap between the potential of your idea and the fallibility of your execution shows you have the judgment you'll need to get better. Although you may not have a remedy for the flaws in your work just yet, being able to identify them is the first step in being able to iron them out. Counterintuitive though it may seem, the fact that the Demon of Disappointment is even at your desk or in your studio reflects well on you. As the Booker Prize-winning author Anne Enright has observed, 'Only bad writers think that their work is really good.'

And isn't it all a question of perspective anyway?

When you put the full stop on the final verse of your poem yesterday, it was a work of genius.

Today, it's doggerel. The truth of course is, most likely, somewhere in between. While it may not be as great as you thought then, it's probably not as bad as it seems now.

Remember that the Demon of Disappointment can only ever afflict the one who envisaged the work in the first place. It's in the eye of the creator, not the beholder. As the creator, you've been working behind the scenes; you know how messy and haphazard the construction was. You've been there when the whole edifice looked as if it were about to collapse in on itself. Yet in spite of all that, you kept going. And now, for better or worse, the work stands on its own, waiting for an audience. That audience, when they come, won't know how the work existed in your imagination; they can only experience the work as it is now, and they will bring all kinds of unexpected nuances to it and make the work anew.

The Demon of Disappointment is a cunning adversary. He's well aware that the reason you became a creator in your medium is because you love that medium. He knows that, as an aficionado, you've sought out the greatest works of all time in your genre. So one of his meanest tricks is to hold up your pedestrian meanderings against the transcendent achievements of the greats, hopeful that the chasm in quality will be enough to deter you from the path of art forever.

But what if you narrow the field of view?

What if you compare your latest work not against the greats, but simply against your own? And you use this comparison as an incentive to make more work?

Let me take you away from the travails of the 21st century and back to the rarefied atmosphere of Japan at the turn of the 19th century. Working in the city of Edo, later Tokyo, is an eccentric and inventive artist whose name is Katsushika Hokusai – also known as Gakyōjin or 'madman of art'. Hokusai has a style that is his own. He blends classical Japanese illustrative techniques with Western principles of perspective, and his creativity is unbridled. He is always painting, making pictures on any flat surface he can find. He works at any scale, from grains of rice to giant, 240-metre-square canvases. He paints street life, birds, fish, plants, landscapes, caricatures, monsters, emperors and paupers. Every day is devoted to work. At one point his studio burns to the ground and his archive is destroyed. He keeps on working. His profligate grandson gambles away the family's money and Hokusai is forced to live in the grounds of a temple. Yet he keeps on working. By the time of his death, the artist is thought to have made more than 30,000 prints, drawings and paintings.

His motivation through all this was simple: he observed that the disparity between what he saw with his eyes and what he painted with his hand was getting smaller, if only by the tiniest of margins, whenever he lifted his brush.

Towards the end of his life he wrote, 'I have drawn things since I was six. All that I made before the age of 65 is not worth counting. At 73 I began to understand the true construction of animals, plants, trees, birds, fishes and insects. At 90 I will enter into the secret of things. At 110, everything – every dot, every dash – will live.'

In the end, Hokusai only made it to 88 and even then, on his deathbed, he is said to have exclaimed, 'If only heaven will give me just another ten years… just another five more years, then I could become a real painter.'

For Hokusai, it was the awareness of his own fallibility that sustained him. Rather than allowing his shortcomings to throw him off course, he used the knowledge that they would gradually diminish as the motivation to keep going.

Life as a creator is tough. Sure, there are those wondrous moments when your muse chooses to smile upon you and your artwork acquires a quality that seems beyond your talent. These rare moments of ecstasy will buoy you along. But most of the time, it's a discouraging trudge around the perimeter of your own limitations as an artist, and an ongoing war of attrition with the Demon of Disappointment.

If you're living through this agony now, know that it's a feeling you share with anyone who has ever sought to give life to their ideas — it's a feeling known even to your artistic heroes — and the most important thing you can do, as Curtis Mayfield once sang, is to keep on keeping on. Because to create is the better part of what makes us human beings human. And though it may not feel like it, the gap between the wonders of your imagination and your ability to render them on the page is getting smaller, with every stroke of your brush, with every tap on your keyboard, with every mark made by your pen.

Epilogue

I feel we know each other a little now, so I'd like to make a confession – a confession that may seem somewhat naive given the subject matter of the last 160 pages or so – I had no idea how hard writing this book was going to be. It was eerie how, with every chapter I wrote, I found myself face to face with the very demon being described.

I put off beginning the first chapter about procrastination for ages. Once under way, I was immediately afflicted with doubt – would I ever make it to the end? And even if I did, who was I to believe that my writing would be worth reading? I ended up in a staring contest with a blank page more times than I'd like to admit. I struggled against the limitations of having to write in a locked-down household during a pandemic, tucked away at the side of a staircase. The dispiriting blow of disappointment was usually the first emotion when I re-read the previous day's scribblings. And I'm sure that any scrupulous reader will no doubt have spotted a mistake or two.

Even with all the hours I'd put into reading, researching and interviewing some of our most eminent creative minds, even being the beneficiary of all their experience and hard-won insights into the creative process, I was still unable to avoid bumping into one demon after another, almost round every bend.

And that's the thing about creative demons.
They can never be completely slain. They are an
extension of ourselves, alter egos, which is why
I've referred to them in this book, written from my
own experience, as 'he'. You can, as we now know,
deflect your demons' most piercing barbs and
protect yourself from their most mischievous wiles,
but as we've also seen, there can be benefits to
having them around.

Accidents, theft, criticism, disappointment, doubt
and even failure can all enhance the creative
process if channelled in the right way.

So, on reflection, maybe the title of this book isn't
quite right.

Instead of *Creative Demons and How to Slay Them*,
maybe it should be *Creative Demons and How to
Learn to Live with Them Because Even Though
It Doesn't Seem Like It at The Time They Are an
Inescapable and Important Part of You Getting to
Make the Creative Work You Want to Make.*

But that wouldn't be quite as snappy, would it?

Thanks for reading this book. I hope you enjoyed it.
Good luck on your next creative journey.

Oh, and if you happen to meet a creative demon,
say 'hi' from me.

Notes

pp. 6–7 'From the point of view': *Infinity Net: The Autobiography of Yayoi Kusama*, English edition © Tate Enterprises Ltd 2011

pp. 14–15 'Faire et se taire': Gustave Flaubert, letter to Miss Amélie Bosquet, 20 August 1866. I'm grateful to the writer Helen Simpson for originally making me aware of this quote – she has it written on a Post-it on the wall by her desk as a stirring reminder whenever the Demon of Procrastination pays a visit.

p. 19 'I'm not a writer': John Steinbeck, *Working Days*, 1990

p. 19 'My painting is dead': Gail Mazur, *Zeppo's First Wife*, 2005

p. 20 'Today you are you': Dr Seuss, *Happy Birthday to You!*, 2005

p. 23 'like driving a car': E.L. Doctorow, 'The Art of Fiction', 1986

p. 24 'People feel that': Martin Gayford, *Modernists and Mavericks*, 2018

pp. 28–29 'If I knew': Paul Zollo, *Songwriters on Songwriting*, Cambridge, MA: Da Capo Press, 2003

p. 31 'You don't know how': Vincent van Gogh, letter dated 2 October 1884, *The Letters of Vincent van Gogh*, 1996

p. 36 'Men of lofty genius': Walter Isaacson, *Leonardo da Vinci: The Biography*, 2017

p. 37 'Slow walking leads': https://www.theguardian.com/books/ng-interactive/2020/nov/07/caught-in-times-current-margaret-atwood-on-grief-poetry-and-the-past-four-years

p. 37 For the 2014 study, see Marily Oppezzo and Daniel L. Schwartz, 'Give Your Ideas Some Legs: The Positive Effect of Walking on Creative Thinking', *Journal of Experimental Psychology: Learning, Memory and Cognition*, 2014, 40 (4), 1142–1152

p. 39 'You don't make the fish': David Lynch, *Catching the Big Fish*, 2006

p. 39 'I always feel': https://www.bbc.co.uk/programmes/m000bxpd

p. 39 'Ideas don't come from': https://www.instagram.com/rickrubin/

p. 40 'the edge of the abyss' and 'At the point of giving up': Brian Eno, *A Year with Swollen Appendices*, 2020

pp. 46–47 'Imagine what you would do': Musa Okwonga, *In The End, It Was All About Love*, Aylesbury: Rough Trade Books, 2021

p. 53 'At such times': Oliver Sacks, *The River of Consciousness*, 2017

p. 55 'Every object conceals another': Brian Eno, *A Year with Swollen Appendices*, 2020

pp. 60–61 'In the beginner's mind': Shunryū Suzuki, *Zen Mind, Beginner's Mind*, Boulder, CO: Shambhala Publications, 2011

p. 68 For more information on the 2021 research paper, see 'People Systematically Overlook Subtractive Changes', www.nature.com

p. 69 'children's performance in creativity tests tends to drop as they get older': see '8 Exercises to Quickly Boost Creative Thinking in Teams', www.medium.com

p. 72 'If you feel safe': https://www.youtube.com/watch?v=cNbnef_eXBM&ab_channel=StuartSemple

p. 72 'ask yourself an interesting enough question': Joe Fig, *Inside the Painter's Studio*, 2009

pp. 76–77 'Every wall is a gate': Ralph Waldo Emerson, *The Complete Works of Ralph Waldo Emerson*, 2006

p. 84 'Maurice, what *can* you draw?': Katie Roiphe, *The Violet Hour*, 2016

p. 85 'we stopped identifying': https://medium.com/@halkirkland_53414/limitation-breeds-innovation-embrace-it-9539db2b5d64

p. 85 'You don't have to let': https://www.telegraph.co.uk/travel/arts-and-culture/agoraphobic-traveller-instagram-google-street-view-photography/

p. 86 'college students were tasked to come up with a new invention': This experiment was cited in Patricia Stokes, 'Variability, Constraints and Creativity', *American Psychologist*, April 2001

pp. 92–93 'To avoid criticism': attributed to Elbert Hubbard

p. 95 'When you're in the studio': https://www.youtube.com/watch?v=h8eczPx7OZo&ab_channel=itsmethecmp

p. 96 'Mr Presley has no': Jack Gould, *New York Times*, 6 June 1956

p. 98 'If I'd been going': Dr Seuss, *The Annotated Cat*, 2007

p. 98 'Can't act. Can't sing': cited in Leslie Halliwell, *The Filmgoer's Book of Quotes*, London: Hart-Davis MacGibbon, 1973

p. 101 'You can't let it go out like that': Laurent Bouzereau, *Hitchcock, Piece by Piece*, 2010

p. 101 'four people who have given': 'Alfred Hitchcock Accepts the AFI Life Achievement Award in 1979', https://www.youtube.com/watch?v=pb5VdGCQFOM&t=194s

p. 102 'When people tell you': https://www.theguardian.com/books/2010/feb/20/ten-rules-for-writing-fiction-part-one

p. 102 'try to read your own': https://www.theguardian.com/books/2010/feb/20/10-rules-for-writing-fiction-part-two

pp. 106–7 'Everyone who you could': Jeff Tweedy, *How to Write One Song*, London: Faber & Faber, 2020

p. 112 For further information on the 2018 study, see 'Reconstructing the Neanderthal Brain Using Computational Anatomy', www.nature.com

p. 113 'As if there was much': Mark Twain, *Twain's Letters*, 2014

p. 114 'I invented nothing new': Anthony Brandt and David Eagleman, *The Runaway Species*, 2017

p. 114 'shameless about stealing great ideas': https://www.youtube.com/watch?v=PdTXS32nAQk

p. 115 'a feeding frenzy': https://www.theredhandfiles.com/originality-hard-to-obtain/

p. 116 'It's not where you take': https://fs.blog/2020/04/shoulders-of-giants/

pp. 120–21 'Nothing is ever planned': https://www.bbc.co.uk/iplayer/episode/m000nx23/maggi-hambling-making-love-with-the-paint

p. 125 'the greatest things in movies': 'They'll Love Me When I'm Dead', Netflix, 2018

p. 127 'If you think': https://www.theguardian.com/books/2020/oct/04/hilary-mantel-wolf-hall-mantel-pieces

p. 128 'there is no other': https://www.bbc.co.uk/programmes/m000p6wd

p. 129 'It could be "apple"': Joe Fassler, *Light the Dark*, 2017

pp. 134–35 'Sometimes A Fuck Up': Darby Hudson, *100 Points of ID to Prove I Don't Exist*, self-published, https://www.etsy.com/listing/947245231/100-points-of-id-paperback

p. 139 'tiny, terrified space of rightness': https://www.ted.com/talks/kathryn_schulz_on_being_wrong?language=en

p. 140 'The history of being': Steven Johnson, *Where Good Ideas Come From*, 2010

p. 143 'the trash can is a treasure trove': Marina Abramović, *Walk Through Walls*, 2016

p. 144 'Miles paused for a second': https://www.youtube.com/watch?v=FL4LxrN-iyw&ab_channel=SafaJah

pp. 150–51 'There's only one thing': Gustav Janouch, *Conversations with Kafka*, 2012

p. 154 'If only I could do this': John Steinbeck, *Working Days*, 1990 p.154 'You know that sickening feeling': https://www.theguardian.com/books/2010/feb/20/10-rules-for-writing-fiction-part-two

p.155 'There is no success': Kae Tempest, *On Connection*, 2020

p.155 'Only bad writers': https://www.theguardian.com/books/2010/feb/20/ten-rules-for-writing-fiction-part-one

p.158 'I have drawn things': https://www.bbc.co.uk/programmes/b08w9lv6

Further Reading

Abramović, Marina, *Walk Through Walls: A Memoir*, London: Penguin Books, 2016

Andreasen, Nancy C., *The Creative Brain: The Science of Genius*, New York: Plume, 2006

Bouzereau, Laurent, *Hitchcock, Piece by Piece*, New York and London: Abrams, 2010

Brandt, Anthony, and Eagleman, David, *The Runaway Species: How Human Creativity Remakes the World*, Edinburgh: Canongate, 2017

Camus, Albert, *Create Dangerously*, London: Penguin, 2018

Cave, Nick, The Red Hand Files (www.theredhandfiles.com)

Csikszentmihalyi, Mihaly, *Creativity: Flow and the Psychology of Discovery and Invention*, HarperCollins, New York: 1996

Csikszentmihalyi, Mihaly, *Flow: The Psychology of Optimal Experience*, New York: Harper and Row, 1990

Dietrich, Arne, 'The Cognitive Neuroscience of Creativity', *Psychonomic Bulletin & Review*, 2004, 11 (6), 1011–1026

Doctorow, E.L., 'The Art of Fiction', interview by George Plimpton in *Paris Review*, Winter 1986, 94 (101)

Emerson, Ralph Waldo, *The Complete Works of Ralph Waldo Emerson: Natural History of Intellect, And Other Papers...*, Ann Arbor, MI: University of Michigan Library, 2006

Eno, Brian, *A Year with Swollen Appendices: Brian Eno's Diary*, London: Faber & Faber, 2020

Fassler, Joe, *Light the Dark: Writers on Creativity, Inspiration, and the Artistic Process*, New York: Penguin, 2017

Fig, Joe, *Inside the Painter's Studio*, New York: Princeton Architectural Press, 2009

Gayford, Martin, *Modernists & Mavericks: Bacon, Freud, Hockney & the London Painters*, London: Thames & Hudson, 2018

Isaacson, Walter, *Leonardo da Vinci: The Biography*, London: Simon & Schuster, 2017

Janouch, Gustav, *Conversations with Kafka*, New York: New Directions, 2012

Johnson, Steven, *Where Good Ideas Come From: The Natural History of Innovation*, New York: Penguin, 2010

Kent, Corita, and Steward, Jan, *Learning by Heart: Teachings to Free the Creative Spirit*, New York: Allworth Press, 2008

Kessels, Erik, *Failed It! How to turn mistakes into ideas and other advice for successfully screwing up*, London: Phaidon, 2016

King, Stephen, *On Writing: A Memoir of the Craft*, London: Hodder & Stoughton, 2000

Kleon, Austin, *Steal Like An Artist: 10 Things Nobody Told You About Being Creative*, New York: Workman, 2012

Kotler, Steven, and Wheal, Jamie, *Stealing Fire: How Silicon Valley, the Navy SEALs, and Maverick Scientists Are Revolutionizing the Way We Live and Work*, New York: Dey Street Books, 2017

Lynch, David, *Catching the Big Fish: Meditation, Consciousness, and Creativity*, Los Angeles: Bobkind Inc., 2006

Lynch, David, and McKenna, Kristine, *Room to Dream: A Life in Art*, Edinburgh: Canongate, 2018

Mazur, Gail, *Zeppo's First Wife: New and Selected Poems*, Chicago: University of Chicago Press, 2005

Mlodinow, Leonard, *Elastic: Flexible Thinking in a Constantly Changing World*, New York: Penguin Random House, 2018

Okwonga, Musa, *In The End, It Was All About Love*, Aylesbury: Rough Trade Books, 2021

Roiphe, Katie, *The Violet Hour: Great Writers at the End*, London: Virago, 2016

Sacks, Oliver, *The River of Consciousness*, London: Picador, 2017

Saltz, Jerry, *How to be An Artist*, London: Ilex, 2020

Saunders, George, *A Swim in a Pond in the Rain*, London: Bloomsbury, 2021

Sendak, Maurice, *Where the Wild Things Are*, London: Bodley Head, 1967

Seuss, Dr, *The Annotated Cat: Under the Hats of Seuss and his Cats*, with an introduction and annotations by Philip Nel, New York: Random House, 2007

Seuss, Dr, *Happy Birthday to You!*, London: HarperCollins Children's Books, 2005

Schulz, Kathryn, *Being Wrong: Adventures in the Margin of Error*, London: Portobello, 2010

Smith, Patti, *Just Kids*, London: Bloomsbury, 2010

Steinbeck, John, *Working Days: The Journals of The Grapes of Wrath, 1938–1941*, edited by Robert J. DeMott, New York: Penguin Books, 1990

Suzuki, Shunryū, *Zen Mind, Beginner's Mind*, Boulder, CO: Shambhala Publications, 2011

Syed, Matthew, *Rebel Ideas: The Power of Diverse Thinking*, London: John Murray, 2019

Tempest, Kae, *On Connection*, London: Faber & Faber, 2020

Twain, Mark, *Twain's Letters, Volume 2, 1867–1875*, CreateSpace, 2014

Tweedy, Jeff, *How to Write One Song*, London: Faber & Faber, 2020

Van Gogh, Vincent, *The Letters of Vincent van Gogh*, London: Allen Lane, 1996

Wilson, Chris, *Horse Latitudes*, London: Sorika, 2013

Zollo, Paul, *Songwriters on Songwriting*, Cambridge, MA: Da Capo Press, 2003

Acknowledgments

While my name looms large on the cover of this book, it wouldn't be here without the invaluable contributions and support of a number of people, to whom I'd like to say a big hearty thank you.

Thank you to the ever-enthusiastic Nicola Davies: you got this whole ball rolling. Thank you to Jo Lightfoot: without your experience and insights I'm not sure a publisher would have ever taken me seriously. Thank you to Roger, Mohara, Ramon and everyone at Thames & Hudson for the hard work you've done in bringing this book into being. Thank you to Fraser and Alex for making it look great. Thank you to my editor Becky Pearson for your subtle but significant interventions, and the gracious way you delivered them; they've made this text much more elegant than it would otherwise have been. Thank you to my friend, the inestimable Tony Pipes, for being an early reader and reassuring me that the whole thing wasn't gobbledegook. Thank you to Mr Al Murphy for squirting your anarchic scribbles between my pages: I owe you a number of martinis. Thank you to my wife, friend, mentor and inspiration Kate Shooter: none of this would have happened without you. Thank you to the writers, musicians, performers and artists who give their all to make the creative work that sustains us. And, finally, thank you to my creative demons: this book wouldn't have been the same without you.

Seuss, Dr, *The Annotated Cat: Under the Hats of Seuss and his Cats*, with an introduction and annotations by Philip Nel, New York: Random House, 2007

Seuss, Dr, *Happy Birthday to You!*, London: HarperCollins Children's Books, 2005

Schulz, Kathryn, *Being Wrong: Adventures in the Margin of Error*, London: Portobello, 2010

Smith, Patti, *Just Kids*, London: Bloomsbury, 2010

Steinbeck, John, *Working Days: The Journals of The Grapes of Wrath, 1938–1941*, edited by Robert J. DeMott, New York: Penguin Books, 1990

Suzuki, Shunryū, *Zen Mind, Beginner's Mind*, Boulder, CO: Shambhala Publications, 2011

Syed, Matthew, *Rebel Ideas: The Power of Diverse Thinking*, London: John Murray, 2019

Tempest, Kae, *On Connection*, London: Faber & Faber, 2020

Twain, Mark, *Twain's Letters, Volume 2, 1867–1875*, CreateSpace, 2014

Tweedy, Jeff, *How to Write One Song*, London: Faber & Faber, 2020

Van Gogh, Vincent, *The Letters of Vincent van Gogh*, London: Allen Lane, 1996

Wilson, Chris, *Horse Latitudes*, London: Sorika, 2013

Zollo, Paul, *Songwriters on Songwriting*, Cambridge, MA: Da Capo Press, 2003

Acknowledgments

While my name looms large on the cover of this book, it wouldn't be here without the invaluable contributions and support of a number of people, to whom I'd like to say a big hearty thank you.

Thank you to the ever-enthusiastic Nicola Davies: you got this whole ball rolling. Thank you to Jo Lightfoot: without your experience and insights I'm not sure a publisher would have ever taken me seriously. Thank you to Roger, Mohara, Ramon and everyone at Thames & Hudson for the hard work you've done in bringing this book into being. Thank you to Fraser and Alex for making it look great. Thank you to my editor Becky Pearson for your subtle but significant interventions, and the gracious way you delivered them; they've made this text much more elegant than it would otherwise have been. Thank you to my friend, the inestimable Tony Pipes, for being an early reader and reassuring me that the whole thing wasn't gobbledegook. Thank you to Mr Al Murphy for squirting your anarchic scribbles between my pages: I owe you a number of martinis. Thank you to my wife, friend, mentor and inspiration Kate Shooter: none of this would have happened without you. Thank you to the writers, musicians, performers and artists who give their all to make the creative work that sustains us. And, finally, thank you to my creative demons: this book wouldn't have been the same without you.